LOSER

The Two-Talent Servant

Tim Boyd

Loser:
The Two-Talent Servant

© 2022 Tim Boyd
All rights reserved.

ISBN 978-1-948022-28-6

Rainer Publishing
www.RainerPublishing.com
Spring Hill, TN

Printed in the United States of America

Contents

The Parable (Matthew 25:14–30, ESV)

For it will be like a man going on a journey, who called his servants and entrusted to them his property. To one he gave five talents, to another two, to another one, to each according to his ability. Then he went away. He who had received the five talents went at once and traded with them, and he made five talents more. So also, he who had the two talents made two talents more. But he who had received the one talent went and dug in the ground and hid his master's money. Now after a long time the master of those servants came and settled accounts with them. And he who had received the five talents came forward, bringing five talents more, saying, "Master, you delivered to me five talents; here, I have made five talents more." His master said to him, "Well done, good and faithful servant. You have been faithful over a little; I will set you over much. Enter into the joy of your master." And he also who had the two talents came forward, saying, "Master, you delivered to me two talents; here, I have made two talents more." His master said to him, 'Well done, good and faithful servant. You have been faithful over a little; I will set you over much. Enter into the joy of your master." He also who had received the one talent came forward, saying, "Master, I knew you to be a hard man, reaping where you did not sow, and gathering where you scattered no seed, so I was afraid, and I went and hid your talent in the ground. Here, you have what is yours." But his master answered him, "You wicked and slothful servant! You knew I reap where I have not sown and gather where I scattered no seed? Then you ought to have invested my money with the bankers, and at my coming I should have received what was my own with interest. So, take the talent from him and give it to him who has the ten talents. For to everyone who has will more be given, and he will have an abundance. But from the one who has not, even what he has will be taken away. And cast the worthless servant into the outer darkness. In place there will be weeping and gnashing of teeth."

The Talent

Talent: "τάλαντον (talanton), ου (ou), τό (to): n.neu.; ≡ Str 5007— LN 6.82 **a talent of money** (of silver valued at 6,000 days;' wages; gold 180,000 days' wages); BAGD refers to it as a measure of weight (varying from about 57 to 80 lbs.). In any case, vast, rhetorical, hyperbolic amounts of money are meant."[1]

Author's note—Talent does not mean talent like we think of it. It was a measure of money. If someone makes $15.00 an hour and works eight hours per day, one talent of Gold is worth $21,600,000. It truly is a hyperbolic amount of money.

Foreword

"You don't get your lunch delivered to you so you can maximize your time?" We shared a good laugh about it. There is a well-known mega church pastor[2] who shares tips on how to use your time better, and this is one of them. He also suggests having someone pick out your clothes, so you don't get decision fatigue. I'm not making fun of this guy. Clearly, he has accomplished some wonderful things. It brings me back to one of the first "pastor" books I read where the guy said he got a limo and a driver so he could use his commuting time to the max.[3]

Why did we laugh? Because we don't relate in any way to his lifestyle. It is not a judgment thing. When I was in my twenties, I would have coveted that life. However, now as a somewhat pudgy guy in his forties working at a small church, I don't wish for it.

Why?

I'm a two-talent person.

I'm not a five-talent person.

Jesus tells the parable of the talents in Matthew 25:14–30. There were three servants listed. One gets five talents and turns them into five more for the master. Another gets two talents and turns them into two more. The last one gets one talent and buries it. We've heard enough about the first and last servant. What about the middle servant?

This servant hears the same thing as the servant who got five talents.

This book is to encourage all of us two-talent servants.

God is equally as happy with our work as with the work of the guy who has personal chefs and shoppers. It is not more, and it is not less. It is equal.

CHAPTER 1

Two Talents

I came to the realization I'm a "two-talent servant" within the last few years. I guess it started right after I turned forty. I still had potential in my twenties and thirties. Right? If you aren't succeeding in those decades, you still have time. However, at some point potential either needs to be realized or . . . not. My potential was not realized. At least, it was not realized in a way that satisfied me.

"Potential not realized" is the nice way to say it. Here is a better way to say it. When I turned forty, I realized I was a loser. No one called me a loser. No one even alluded to it. In fact, it was quite the opposite. Pretty much everybody in my life saw me as a successful person. I remember a conversation I had with a good friend after I had moved to become a lead pastor. The new church was far less prestigious and a lot smaller than the previous one. I was embarrassed by this downward move. I didn't let on that I was. I just joked about how this was only a start for me, and the church would be big and awesome in no time. He said from the outside looking in it looked like I had moved up, from associate to lead. I didn't see it that way. I saw myself as a loser who had not lived up to the potential God had given me. I felt this way for most of my thirties.

Where did this feeling come from? I can't blame teachers, professors, colleagues, etc. My parents never gave me the idea I was not successful. Not one of them said I needed to be a pastor at a megachurch to be successful, even though that is the only way I would feel successful. Well, maybe being a megachurch pastor and a having a book. Well, a book and a speaking tour. Well, I can go on forever. Where did this come from? I can't blame the system, the world, the machine, or whatever else we want to call it. Simply put, it was only me who saw me as a loser.

So, I had to do something with the feeling. I wanted to do something healthy with it. I wanted to take it to God to let his glory shine through it. This book is my journey. I say "my journey" because I am the one on it, but hopefully you will see God as the hero of my story. In my broken and prideful way, I took this to God so he could help me cope with my feelings of failure and inadequacy. He has brought me through an incredible journey of self-discovery, biblical revelation, and big-time freedom and joy. I am happy to lead our little church in this part of God's kingdom. It changed me for the better. This realization has made me a better friend. It changed my marriage and my relationships with my kids. It changed our church. This revelation had to hit me in a couple of ways. I needed to, first, realize I was a loser, and second, to embrace my "loser-ness."

You may think the term loser is going too far. I completely disagree. When I was just out of high school I flunked out of college and moved back to my hometown. I was working the night shift at a warehouse and drinking all day. I didn't like what I was doing and started to realize there was no future to it, so I called up my former youth pastor. We got together and I joked I was a loser. He agreed.[4] I needed someone I respected and someone who loved me to let me know my feeling was correct. His agreement with my assessment led me on a journey back to Jesus. So, when I use the term loser, I mean it in sincerity. By my own definition I was a loser. To God I was not a loser. To my family and friends, I was not a loser. This book is about my inner battle, my pride, and God's incredible patience with me.

I have been on this journey for three or four years now, but it came to a head during my morning devotions[5] on October 18, 2021. This particular morning I read about the servant who was given two talents. There are two other servants listed in that parable, and they get the most attention. I get it. We all love the margins. We love the extremes. The extremes are interesting. However, most of us don't live in the extremes. I read books written by pastors of churches with 50,000 people. It's hard for me to relate to anything they write. I read articles about pastors who have done terrible things in their churches. I also don't relate to anything they are writing. I'm not super successful and I'm not facing an internal investigation. You aren't either. We are the hundreds of thousands of people who live between the extremes. In the parable one servant was super successful, and one servant failed miserably. I had read about and taught about this parable before, but I had not been ready to notice the beauty of being a two-talent servant. The overwhelming majority of us relate best to the two-talent servant.

First, let me share a little bit of my story so you can see where I'm coming from. I'll bet my story isn't too different from yours. You would never have purchased this book if you still thought of yourself as a five-talent servant. Winners don't read books written by nobodies! Right?

I grew up in a pastor's house and we did church stuff all the time. It was great. I loved that life. It was not without its struggles, but I loved the churches we grew up in. My dad was one of the successful pastors in the Dakotas United Methodist Conference. We were at a great church from the time I was in fifth grade through my high school graduation. Attendance averaged around 300–500. It was a very healthy church. My dad always valued having a youth pastor, and I was blessed because of this. I had great youth pastors. Our youth pastors were great people who really cared about us. They did their best to have great programs and because of this I was able to have friends at church.

We went to awesome camps. At one of these camps, I clearly remember an older man who was important in our denomination. He was there to talk with my dad and some other people at the camp. He must have been impressed with me. I was in lower elementary school (so I was completely full of potential), and I remember him saying I would accomplish something great. At this point I want to make a dumb joke, but I can't. Even at an early age I remember how great it made me feel and I knew he must be telling the truth and I knew I would be amazing. I didn't ask any clarifying questions. I have no idea what he meant. I'm guessing I'm not the only kid he told it to. His words became a driving idea in my life. I will accomplish something great. I have to. I believed God made me to accomplish great things.

Through a series of God-inspired events I ended up at a small Bible college in Nebraska. One year before graduation my wife and I were invited to join a church planting team. I was to be the media pastor.[6] I was twenty-one years old, and I was pretty sure I was ready to start accomplishing something great. I didn't know any other "media pastors." For church plants in Minnesota, this one was very successful. The church started with 300 in attendance and just kept climbing. If social media had existed back then, I would have been posting stats every week. A few months in, I preached for the very first time, and one member of the church planting board told my boss I was clearly the next guy to plant the next church. I was twenty-three, and it was probably time for me to be unleashed to the world. Ministry had to happen, and I was arrogant enough to do it well! Due to financial issues with the church plant, my wife and I returned to finish school after working with this very successful church plant after just eighteen months. We had one semester of school left. Once back at school I was the hot prospect on the market for the openings in the area . . . I assumed.

During that semester, a church of about six hundred needed a student pastor, and I decided to stoop down to their level to fill that role. I remember sitting at a vision meeting one night and thinking how lucky they were I worked there. I didn't have the best attitude. Think Peter pre-rooster crowing. I worked as the student pastor for a couple of years while the church grew like crazy and built a brand-new building in a brand-new part of town. In just a few years the church doubled in size, and I accepted a new role as associate pastor and oversaw a team of full-time staff. I had accomplished all this in my twenties. This whole time I was simply trying to build my resume for the megachurch that would one day be lucky enough to have me. I had friends from Bible college who were envious of my position. None of it was good enough for me though.

This church was much different than the church I grew up in. The church I grew up in was made up of people of all ages. You would celebrate parents bringing their babies up to the front so we could all see how cute they were. You would have the old lady who smiles at you all the time. You also had the old lady that scowled at you when you whispered during the services. This church was full of people in their thirties and forties. The church I grew up in occasionally had new people. We had churchwide picnics in the park with fried chicken. Your friend's grandparents were in the congregation. Actually, they were upstairs in the adult classrooms with the comfy chairs. This church was more like a stream of people flooding into it and out of it. You wouldn't put too much stock into people because you feared they would leave soon. I felt that I was constantly training new volunteers to replace the ones that left. The church I grew up in never talked about leadership development or had volunteer "pushes." When I was in fifth grade two men from the church stepped up to teach the fifth-grade Sunday school class because it was so large, and we had so much energy. They were asked to serve, and they did it. They didn't respond to a blurb on social media or attend a training seminar. This church talked about little else. It's as if people were on a conveyer belt to become volunteers who give 10 percent and constantly invite people to church. I felt that there was something wrong with this church. I was far too arrogant to guess that I could be wrong in any way. So, it must have been the church.

I had told the church I would work there for five years, and once those five years ended, I was ready to leave and pursue something better. I left for graduate school. I knew I needed a degree for the jobs awaiting me. At this point my wife and I had three kids, so I needed to work full-time. I decided to take my talents[7] to a church of two hundred people in a town of six hundred people. I felt I was too good for them, which is pretty much the worst way to step into a ministry job. I realized a few things those four years we spent at the small-town church and going to grad school. First, I realized God couldn't use me until I was broken. Second, I realized he loved me enough to let me break.

I wonder how the two-talent servant felt. He had to feel inferior to the five-talent servant. The parable doesn't tell us any more about him. I understand this is all conjecture. However, I just can't imagine he was happy with his two talents. Not after he saw another servant get five. It is a parable of Jesus, so I think it is okay for us to humanize the humans in the story. In doing this, we can really put ourselves into Jesus's teaching to try and experience what he was revealing about God and his kingdom. Jesus preached in parables to explain complex issues. Putting myself into this parable, I wondered, how could this servant handed only two talents not feel bad when he saw the other one with five? After all, I would have been devastated.

If I had never seen a megachurch, maybe I wouldn't have felt like I needed to accomplish this goal. If I had never read a church-growth book or attended a church-growth seminar or heard a podcast from the next guy whose church grew by five thousand in one day—maybe I wouldn't have felt it so much. Right? How many of us would be happy in our churches of fifty, one hundred, two hundred, or five hundred if we weren't right down the road from a church of a thousand, five thousand, or whatever?

I think it's vitally important that we address the issues that we have. If it's envy, we have to look into the mirror and see it in all its ugliness. Professional counseling, sharing with friends, and praying for wisdom and guidance from God are all a valuable part of this process. We can't just ignore these issues though. I was more than just envious. I was dealing with the reality of my own limitations. I had such a hard time dealing with the idea that I was limited in any way that I had to fight myself to avoid falling into a life of lies. If you do any type of counseling or even just have friends and family, then you know of people who have given into their own lies. The guy who continues to believe he was the better quarterback in high school or the lady who just knew if she grew up in a larger town, she would have had a better life. They can't take any responsibility for their perceived failure or lack of forward movement. I was dealing with this, and I'm so glad God didn't let me stay in those lies. This parable lays out the truth that there were three servants given three different amounts from their master.

Honestly, it seems unfair that the servants get a different number of talents. Maybe the previous sentence was not honest. This would be a more honest statement. It didn't seem fair that I didn't get the maximum number of talents.

CHAPTER 2

Pray It into the Stick

T he most successful I felt was in the first couple of years as the youth pastor at the rapidly growing church. I was there during a season of growth. The growth had very little to do with my contribution to the church, but I got the feeling of being successful, and I really enjoyed that.

The highlight of that time was being asked to speak at a camp that was very special to me. This was a camp that I had been to as a camper and as a staff member. Now I was being given the opportunity to do a big boy job. I had been to this weeklong camp twice in high school, worked there a summer after high school, and it was life changing. This camp was in northern Minnesota, just a loon's flight from Lake Superior.[8] Our church would always go in early June, which meant it would still drop into the forties at night when we slept in those tiny little tents. The camp was located on a lake surrounded by trees. The camp itself was beautiful and it was in the most beautiful place in the world. I've often said that God summers up there. It was a leadership camp for kids from the youth ministries of area churches who took their faith seriously and showed some potential. Obviously, it was the camp for me, with a special emphasis on the second part of that last sentence.

This camp was all about living up to your God given potential. It was like a native language to me, and I soaked it all up. The camp was much more like a conference or summer intensive course than a typical camp. Playing games and free time weren't the focus. You weren't there for nonsense. You were there to realize what God had given you and to use that gift to the maximum. At this camp, campers mapped out a life plan. This was both a five-year plan and a plan for your entire life. I loved working on those topics. We did a period of self-reflection followed by a lot of Scripture. Then we did a ton of different trainings, such as gaining skills for having conversations with strangers.[9] It was an intense camp with no wasted time.

There were two highlights to this camp. First, we would go to Split Rock Lighthouse State Park and spend four hours in solitude. You would get the chance to wander around this beautiful place all by yourself. You were encouraged not to talk to anyone or listen to music. Even before cell phones, it was an amazing experience. Those experiences have changed my life and taught me to use solitude in the rhythm of my life now. I spent most of the time thinking about how much God loves me and how awesome he created me. Reflecting on the love God has for us is always life giving and well worth the time. Thinking about how awesome God made you or me doesn't ever lead to peace or benevolence. During our time of solitude, the only assignment we had was to write a letter about our future selves. Mine was filled with success. We would spend the evening on the shores of Lake Superior reading our letters to the rest of the campers. Even then the leaders viewed me as the one with all the potential.

The second highlight of this camp was sharing our life story in front of the whole camp. Every camper, adult leader, and even the camp staff would share. This happened after every meal we ate. Two or three people would get five minutes to share. I excelled with this assignment. Why? Well, I loved attention and I loved talking about myself. It was always a great experience. After you were finished the leader would give the opportunity for three people to encourage you. The summer I worked there, I was challenged by the camp director to change the presentation of my life story. He told me to make God the hero of my story instead of myself. I did it because I knew it would impress people even more. I'm pretty sure that's not what he was going for.

A few years had passed, I was now a youth pastor, and it was my turn to take a handful of students to this camp. I was excited. It took a lot of convincing to get them there. I knew that if I got one group to go, then other groups would follow. I think that first year five students went. It was going to be great! Then the person leading the camp that week called and invited me to give the biggest talk of the camp. I couldn't believe it. It was my first year as an adult leader there and I was already batting cleanup.[10] I was getting the sweet opportunity to speak at the campfire and challenge students to lay their lives down to pick up the life Jesus had for them. Of course, the irony of me speaking on this subject wasn't yet evident. It was the crescendo of the camp experience. It was the big deal part. I was the closer.[11]

And I knocked it out of the park. Wait, I'm mixing baseball metaphors here. Anyways, I did an amazing job. I even exceeded my own lofty expectations.

Seriously, we had kids crying. The adult leaders were rethinking their lives and choices. I was on fire. I started off strong, got stronger through the middle, and ended as strong as the granite along the shores of Lake Superior. It felt like the beginning of a movement.

At this point in my life, I was under the impression I was a five-talent guy. I would be a ten-talent guy, but Jesus didn't go high enough in the story. If I had been around, maybe he would have. This was the pinnacle of my perceived success. I'm not overstating this either. I can still identify that moment as the moment I felt the most ungodly pride I've ever felt. Do you have a moment like this? I'm sure you do. I can now recognize how gracious it was of God to not let me get the success I think I wanted. I'm certain it would have ruined me. It's the whole "child-star phenomenon." I wouldn't wish too much success too quickly on anyone. It's too much pressure and they aren't ready for it. Why did God choose to be so gracious to me? I don't know. However, I wonder if it has to do with our parable. Did he see me as a servant who could only handle two talents? So out of his wisdom and love did he only bless me with two instead of three? I didn't have any of those thoughts at that time. I believed I was on the fast track to be the next big thing.

It is amazing to think God was still using me. I was doing my best to build my own kingdom, and God was still letting me serve in his. I feel like I was the living example of the old phrase "if God only used perfect people, he wouldn't use any of us." Looking back at this, it is hard for me to not be embarrassed. However, it is even harder not to recognize the love of God. His love is evident through his patience with me. Why didn't he just let me self-implode? Why did he graciously continue to guide me and accomplish his work through me? Because he is perfect, and his love is perfect.

Here is how my teaching went. I started off humblebragging about my life. I was a youth pastor at a rapidly growing church in a major metro area (bigger than any of the cities that the other people at the camp lived in). I had just bought my first minivan.[12] I had several shirts with snaps.[13] My wife was beautiful, and I had a couple really cute kids. I had just bought a house. It was like I was going after Paul's boasting in 2 Corinthians 11. You preach well? I preach better. You look cool? I look cooler. Your church is large? Mine is larger. You think you are awesome? I'm awesome! What was I supposed to be talking about? Oh yeah, give it all up for Jesus!

In a masterful stroke I told everyone around the campfire to pick up a stick and pray their dreams into the stick.[14] I said to take all the plans you have for your future, visualize them, and then visualize putting them into the stick. Then take the stick and toss it into the fire. This is to symbolize you throwing away your dreams for what God would have for you.

The problem?

I thought God's dreams would be better—as defined by me— versions of my dreams. If I thought I would preach at a church of ten thousand, it meant God would bring me to a church of fifty thousand. Where did this idea come from? Was I just an arrogant kid, or was there more to it? There was more to it. I had the sin of pride in my life, but gasoline got poured on that fire. That gas was consumer Christianity and the church-growth movement. I was entering into ministry at a time when we saw the rise of celebrity pastors. The culture created the celebrity pastor. I gave into this idea. I assumed that I needed to lead a large church, write a book, and do a tour. This is how it had to go. Anything less than this would be failure.

I never entertained the idea of failure. I knew I would get what I wanted, and it would always be even better than what I thought I wanted. It probably didn't help I was reading books by Robert Shuler.[15] I preached a message in direct opposition to how I was living, yet I didn't pick up on the irony.

That talk was delivered twenty-five years ago. I prayed into that stick twenty-five years ago. I've lived more years on this side of the stick. I still have a minivan, but it is nicer. I have a larger house. My wife is still beautiful, and I have even more really cute kids. I no longer have shirts with snaps, but I have three pairs of Jordans, a pair of British Knights,[16] and a 1994 Honda Del Sol. I'm a little pudgier. The last eight years I've been leading a church that hasn't become a megachurch. I'm not a famous speaker. I haven't done amazing things for God. This book may never be published. Twenty-five years later I truly did pray those dreams into the stick not realizing God's answer would be much different than what I was anticipating.

I wonder what it would be like to meet the kid who wrote the letter about how awesome his life was going to be. I wonder what he would think of me now. Actually, I know exactly what he would think of me now. I guarantee he would think I'm a loser. He would think I don't have what it takes. He would see me now as some normal, small-church pastor who isn't good enough to succeed. He would attribute this assessment to lack of skill, talent, hard work, or faith. In his blind ambition, self-absorption, and lack of wisdom he wouldn't see me as filled with far more faith than he was. He wouldn't see me (and you and thousands of us) fighting the good fight with all our strength every day. He wouldn't see the success of a saved marriage in our little church or all the other things he would say are the ways "losers celebrate being losers."

You know what else he wouldn't see?

He wouldn't see a person who found the freedom that came from the realization he is a two-talent guy. The younger version of me was filled with anxiety, frustration, and pain. Ha! It's nice to be older and have more time walking with Jesus. This older, pudgier version of me is filled with peace, joy, and freedom. It is awesome. None of this would have happened if God didn't answer my prayer of taking all the selfish dreams I prayed into the stick and replacing them with his dreams. God answered prayer for me in his unbelievable grace and kindness.

God answered my selfish prayer by leading me through a painful journey. I don't believe God made the journey painful. The journey was painful because of me and my pride. My pride had to be dealt with. Someone wrote, "God sends his children to school in the wilderness." That person was right on in my experience. I had no idea just how hard the wilderness would be and how long the experience would last. I'm certain you've had a wilderness experience as well, and I'm certain you wouldn't want to do it over again, yet you count yourself blessed with all the wisdom you have because of it.

In the parable there is no mention of the attitude or makeup of the two-talent or five-talent servants. We only see the results of their faithfulness with what the master had given them. We don't get the timeframe. We have no idea how long it took. This is what we know: "For it will be like a man going on a journey, who called his servants and entrusted to them his property" (Matthew 25:14). I think we can make the jump that this is what we are called to in life. Jesus has gone on ahead to prepare a place. He will come back. In the meantime, we (his servants) are entrusted with the work. This was not my view at the time. I believed I had a great work to accomplish. I was missing the whole "entrusted with his property" part. Graciously, he taught me all about it.

CHAPTER 3

Bloom Where You're Planted

So, we moved to a small church in a small town, and it went south in the first month. I brought the city to the country, and it was not a good fit. This church wanted to reach young people, so it hired a young pastor. I'm not saying it can't work. However, if it is the only thing a church is willing to do to reach young people, then it will fail. I was thirty and still had some time left before I was too old for "potential." So, I was a solo pastor. I know God had called us there. I know he wanted us there. I thought he wanted us there so the church there could grow numerically. I believed the biggest measure of success was the growth of attendance. I saw everything else as secondary to that goal. It is what I picked up from the first two churches I worked at. It is also what I picked up from the church-growth culture of America at the time. It is not what I was learning at graduate school. Graduate school was teaching me something entirely different.

One of my duties as a small-town pastor was visiting people in nursing homes. I understand they are called something else now. I would visit one lady every two to three weeks. She hated it there. I didn't love it there either. She was grumpy. I tried to do my best to stay there for a full hour. Generally, the hour would be the same. She would complain about all the same things over and over. She would never break eye contact as she went through her list of complaints. They stretched through her ninety-plus years on earth.

The place itself was not bad. The people were nice. The facilities were clean and updated. She had a wonderful view of a tree and the park. I really did like her view. None of those mattered to her. She didn't like being there. She had a picture a child had colored for her on one of her closet doors. It read "bloom where you're planted." She was not blooming there. Her name was Fern. The joke writes itself.

She didn't like it there, and she was not going to bloom where she was planted. She didn't want to be there and was not going to change. She blamed her kids for putting her there. She didn't realize how hard it was for them to put her there. They simply couldn't take care of her how she needed. She needed to look for God there and make the best of the situation. She needed to find life there. She needed to be able to find some joy and peace in the place she was. She needed to bloom where she was planted. Looking back now I wonder, how did I not see myself in her situation? I was going through the same thing. God had placed me somewhere, and I was refusing to bloom. I wonder how much good could have happened if I would have bloomed where I was planted. I did try during the first few months but quickly realized I was not willing to invest my life into the community. Did this mean I had taken the talent God had given me and buried it? Wait—am I only a one-talent servant???

At this point in my life, I had only bloomed in one of the three churches I was planted. Oddly enough, it was a church plant. I loved it there and thought I would retire with this church. I poured myself into church and into my job. It was the only place I gave everything I had to accomplish the work I was called to do. The other two places I served I was somewhat reserved with blooming, because I didn't want to waste a good bloom on a poor planter. I felt as though those churches where not going to be the place I landed. They were transitionary, so I held back. This resulted in about a ten-year period in which I was more like the one-talent servant.

I think that guy buried his talent in the ground because he was too worried about himself and his career. I could relate.

Then the man who had received one bag of gold came. "Master," he said, "I knew you are a hard man, harvesting where you have not sown and gathering where you have not scattered seed. So I was afraid and went out and hid your gold in the ground. See, here is what belongs to you." (Matthew 25:24–25)

He said, "I was afraid." So was I. I was afraid I was a one-talent servant. I was afraid my potential would never be realized or, even worse, that I didn't have potential. So, I spent a lot of time trying to prove myself or stick up for myself. I was worried about my career arc. Honestly, I took my first promotion because I didn't want my kids to be embarrassed their dad was only a student pastor. At the time they were all under six. They weren't super focused on my career arc. I probably took my first senior pastor job for the same reason. I didn't feel successful, so I was afraid I might never be successful.

I was so focused on myself I never would have been able to handle the next part of this Scripture. It is so much worse than just feeling like a failure. The master has very harsh words for the one-talent servant. Even worse than those words is what the master does. He throws the servant out into the darkness.

> His master replied, "You wicked, lazy servant! So, you knew I harvest where I have not sown and gather where I have not scattered seed? Well then, you should have put my money on deposit with the bankers, so when I returned I would have received it back with interest." So take the bag of gold from him and give it to the one who has ten bags. For whoever has will be given more, and they will have an abundance. Whoever does not have, even what they have will be taken from them. And throw that worthless servant outside, into the darkness, where there will be weeping and gnashing of teeth."

I didn't realize just how far out of God's will and work I was. I was so focused on my version of success that I was not following God. I was going to graduate school and pastoring a church. I was reading the Bible, praying, and serving. I was doing my best to be an encouraging husband and wise father. Yet I still was not following God. I was doing things I thought would lead to my success. I wanted to be everything God wanted me to be, but I also wanted God to know what I thought I should be.

I wonder if he looked at me as I look at my five-year-old son. He will routinely tell me what he is. One day he is a ninja. One day he is a YouTuber. One day he is a policeman, etc. He really pours himself into those roles. He goes outside to our front lawn and talks on his little walkie talkie and even writes tickets as cars drive by. Yet, when I watch him, I don't believe he is any of those things. In fact, I don't care if he is any of those things. I just want him to realize his potential. I want him to live his fullest life like what Jesus promises in John 10:10. You know life to the full through him? To me, his earthly success doesn't matter. Also, it is age appropriate to think that way. I was no longer a kindergartner. I needed to grow up.

God didn't give up on me though. He took me to school in the wilderness. Over the four years I served a small church in a small town I was broken a little more every month. I walked into the job an arrogant, prideful (wicked?) servant, and I limped out of there a broken, fearful, and weary servant. Things got so bad I wanted to leave many times. I even wanted to leave the ministry. God wouldn't let me. Seriously, I applied for other jobs, and no one wanted me. I had to work for God because no one else wanted to hire me. At one point things had gotten so rough that I was talking to my dad on the phone and told him I just couldn't take much more and would quit if I had the money to quit. He responded, "Well, do you love them?" He was referring to the people in the little church in the little town. I was embarrassed to admit I had never thought of that.

My dad brought up an amazing point. To get back to the parable, I had been "entrusted with the master's property." I was not doing this. I was not focused on the property I was to take care of. Worse, I was not focused on the master. The answer should have been that I do love them because God has called me there to love them. He loves them, and therefore I will love them.

I am a firm believer love is found and nurtured in commitment. I was not committed to them and did not love them well. I think the two-talent servant and five-talent servant served their master because they loved him. They didn't want to misuse his property. They wanted to prove faithful. I didn't want to prove faithful. I wanted to prove successful. The master doesn't say "well done, good and successful servant." Jesus chose the word faithful. If I'm chasing success, it is all up to me. If I'm chasing faithfulness, then success is up to God.

I didn't bloom where I was planted, and it was completely my fault. I had buried the talent I was entrusted with right in the ground. I was just sitting there biding my time and hating my life. I was a loser and a failure and all the potential I thought I once had must have been a lie. God started to answer the prayer I prayed years before. You know the dumb prayer about praying my dreams into a stick and throwing them into the fire so I can live God's dreams? I didn't realize then that God played the long game. He had given me two talents, and he was going to help me use them.

Conversely, going to graduate school was a gift from God. I needed to be learning while I was being schooled in that small town. I attended my classes once a week. It was a nice two-hour drive each way across the prairie of middle Illinois. I would listen to sermons on the way up and podcasts on the way home. I would sit in these classes with other men and women going through many of the same things. As arrogant as I was at my job, I was humble at school. I had to take Hebrew. I couldn't get it. I studied all the time. I met with my faculty advisor, and he told me flatly, "Some people just don't get language." The common theme of every class, every professor, and every book I was assigned to read was faithful obedience to God. They taught a honing of skill instead of a display of talent. I read about healthy church growth as opposed to win-at-all-costs church growth. In a way, going to school and developing relationships with other students and professors kept me in the ministry through the tumultuous time we had in that small town church.

Nevertheless, I was not blooming where I was planted. I took what God had given me, and I was doing very little with it. I had tried. I might have oversold how arrogantly I walked into that job. It's true that I did want it to grow numerically, but I honestly wanted people to find and follow Jesus. I really did try at times. I didn't fight back when I was struck. I didn't gossip when I was gossiped about. Those are two of my greatest accomplishments at that church. I did not misrepresent myself or misrepresent Jesus by fighting, arguing, and quarreling. It's like I wanted to bury the talent in the ground, and I wanted to use the talents for my master. I wanted to bury it because I was sick of confrontation and feeling like everyone doubted everything I did. I wanted to just give up and find somewhere else to work. However, I wanted to use the talents because I saw people in that church and community who were growing, who were reaching out to people in God's name, and who wanted to see their church be the church that Jesus had in mind.

I wonder if the one-talent servant was fearful the entire time or just part of the time. Was there an internal struggle going on? Did he race back to the place he buried the talent just to make sure it was still there? Did he think about much? It's a parable, so we don't know. It's a parable, so it's okay to spend time thinking about this question. I would assume that right away he was afraid and buried it in the ground.

I imagine there are two extremes to his thoughts about this talent as time went on. The first extreme is he thought about it less and less. He was so selfish that he spent his time thinking about his own stuff instead of the master's stuff. Fear and pride together are a dangerous combination. Ask the followers of King Saul. Pride doesn't always look like a puffed-out chest and too many pictures on social media. Kyle Idleman preached, "Insecurity is just pride pointed inwards." That's the better way to look at insecurity. Generally, in the church world, we look at insecurity as a humility or meekness. Then we hold that up as being godly. But insecurity is not humility; it's pride. Pride is a sin. Humility isn't feeling bad about yourself. Humility is having a correct estimation of yourself. Humility is knowing what you are good and what you aren't good at.

Humility is knowing God made you and gave you ability. Humility is the key to understanding where you fit in in the master's kingdom and where you fit in in your local church.

Meekness is not insecurity either. We read "blessed are the meek for they will inherit the earth" (Matthew 5:5), and we picture Adrian from the Rocky movies.[17] She is quiet and shy and has no confidence at all. That's insecurity, not meekness. Meek in the Greek is humble, gentle, and mild. Those aren't weak characteristics. To be gentle and mild is incredible strength. For instance, I desire to be meek when I'm driving my car. Then I will be able to handle being cut off without yelling and losing my cool. It doesn't mean that I don't care or am insecure; it means that I am secure enough to not let it dictate my response and behavior.

This servant hid the talent and over time forgot all about it. That is a shame. He could have used that talent for the master's glory and spent his days on the ride of his life. That's what he missed. He missed out on life. He missed out on being witness to the master's talents being doubled. He missed out on so much joy and peace that he would have received doing the master's work. He didn't get that. He didn't bloom where he was planted.

The second extreme response is that the servant thought about the talent in the ground all the time. He went out and buried the talent because he was afraid, and then he couldn't quit thinking about it. It's like he could hear the thumping sound come up from the floorboards like Edgar Allen Poe's narrator in the "Tell-Tale Heart." It haunted him. He woke up at night wondering when the master would come back and what he would think. He went back often to make sure no one had dug it up. Fear drove him to inaction, yet his mind stayed very active.

We call this worry. We also call it anxiety. Of course, Jesus also teaches on worry. He picks a few of the more common things that many of us worry about and says that God will take care of all these things. He doesn't leave it there, though. He continues to give us something to do with that energy we were previously using for worry. In the Sermon on the Mount we read, "But seek first His kingdom and His righteousness, and all these things will be given to you as well" (Matthew 6:33). There is something for you and me to do.

The servant that buries the talent now has nothing to do but worry. The life that he was meant to lead is buried there in the ground, and he was the one who did it. He loses the joy and peace that come from being in the will of God. He worries, and he should worry. He is destined to be thrown out to the place to where there is wailing and gnashing of teeth. The master will return, and he should be afraid.

What could he do differently? I relate to the servant's fear. I assume we all relate to being fearful of accomplishing the master's work. He completely screws it up because he doesn't do the correct thing with that fear. He needs to take that fear to God. Here's where the parable breaks down a bit for my pontification. Could the servant just have called the master to ask for some advice and reassurance? I don't know. I do know that you and I can. Jesus begs us to do this when he says, "Come to me all you who are weary and burdened and I will give you rest" (Matthew 11:28). He doesn't stop there either. He gives us something to do. First, we are to come to him. Then we are to take from him. Finally, we are to learn from him. Then we will find rest for our souls. We come to him and take His yoke and learn from him. A yoke was a particular set of teachings from a Rabbi. In this case, we would take Jesus's teachings on life and carry them out. Then we find that his yoke, or way of living, is easy and light. Worrying is neither easy nor light. If he was full of fear and worry, then he was not blooming where he was planted.

God had given me two talents, and he was going to help me use them. Just about the time I had this realization is when God told my wife it was okay for us to leave the little church. I'm pretty sure I started sending out resumes the minute after she told me we could move. I sent them to a bunch of larger churches for pretty much any position they had. I only asked for two things. First, I didn't want to be the lead pastor. Second, I didn't want to work at a small church. I may have thrown the stick in the fire, but I wanted to make sure it didn't burn completely.

So, we moved to Florida so I could be the lead pastor at a small church. Ugh.

CHAPTER 4

Oak Tree or Machine?

We moved to Florida in July. It was hot. It stayed hot every single day for about the last eight years. It's not just hot like the Midwest. It's the kind of heat that makes you angry at first. Then you just choose to accept its oppressiveness and learn to live with sweating between every door. You sweat when you leave the house on the way to your car. You sweat in your car until the AC really gets going. Then you sweat from your car to the office. Then you have a meeting with another person who has broken a sweat three times that day already. It's fun.[18]

In addition to the oppressive heat, I also had no idea what I was getting into with the church. I was told the church was about 250 people and a little bigger in the winter due to the snowbirds (the people live in the Midwest in the summer and Florida in the winter). The attendance my first Sunday was right around 125 people total. What they should have told me is the church was 250 about ten years before my arrival. I knew the church was small, but I didn't realize just how small. However, the size of the church was not the real struggle.

The first three years I was the lead pastor were full of conflict that had been bubbling under the surface for more than a decade. I didn't realize it at the time, but God sent me to a small church in a small town to prepare me to lead this church in Florida. He had truly sent to me to school in the wilderness. It was uncanny to see all I had learned through school and my previous church was so pertinent to what had been happening in this church. It was the same church in a different location. I thought I was getting away from the conflict and problems. This goes to prove you can never really run from your problems. I thought I was being released. I was simply being moved into a different war zone. The problems, power struggles, and obstacles we couldn't overcome at church were the same ones God brought me to Florida to lead through. Once again, I'm shocked that I didn't see the similarities at the time. This church, like the previous church, also wanted to hire a young pastor to reach young families. Once again, they weren't willing to change anything else in the church other than the age of the pastor.

I'm sure this doesn't fit the parable of the servants, but it was like God wouldn't let me bury my talent in the ground. I had been looking for ways to get out of the ministry but hadn't found any. The first few years at the church in Florida were the same. I have never been offered a ministry job. Each one that I've had is because I applied for it and went through the interview process. In my more than twenty-year career, no one has wanted to hire me to work at their church. I have also never been offered a secular job. This shocks the part of me that still feels like a five-talent servant. This makes sense to the part of me that has accepted being a two-talent servant. This is crushing to the part of me that identifies with the one-talent servant.

I think it's God's special provision for me that I haven't been offered any other job, church, or secular. I am certain that God knows I would have taken the offered jobs and would not be where he wants me to be. I am a professional rationalizer. I can pretty much make any argument to support any decision that I have already made. That is not a strength! Did God make it so I couldn't bury my talent in the ground? I think so. After all, I was praying that his will would be done in my life. He is still answering that prayer. Why? Apparently, he saw potential in me. But I wasn't really burying my talent in the ground; I was using it as though it was mine and it was meant for my glory.

This church was attractive to me. The conversations that I had with the leaders of the church led me to believe we would be able to work together because we had a common understanding and common goals. I was incorrect. I do not believe anyone lied to me during the interview phase, but I think it is very hard to assess ourselves. They had been a part of the church for so long they could not see the glaring problems.

It is kind of like working on my car. Recently my car wouldn't start. I immediately went to Google, Facebook Groups, and YouTube to find out why. Instantly I knew what was wrong, so I replaced the ignition assembly. That didn't fix it. So, I purchased a starter I have yet to install. I changed the fuel filter and a crimp that was in the line.[19] I still was not having any luck. No one told me to do any of these things. I just happened to read about them on the World Wide Web and then decided to do them. Finally, I found out the real problem was a four-dollar switch. Had I asked someone for help, I might have saved myself a few hundred dollars and three full weekends. Like me, the church leaders were looking for answers but not asking for help.

While I was making up my mind, I saw many positives about this church. They had everything paid off. They did not have very much money, but at least they weren't in debt at all. They had a pretty good footprint in a neighborhood. They had just gone through a miserable failure, and it made them realize they needed help. They seemed fun.

Finally, I was convinced on taking this position was when the leaders of the church said they wanted to reach the neighborhood. (You may think the reason is that the church is seven miles from the beach. Honestly, I hate the weather here. I'm a guy who loves seasons and open prairies.) I thought it was a great plan to be a part of. Also, I was pretty sure I could help them do it. I was ready to use my five talents. Once again, I thought I knew what needed to happen, and God allowed me to fumble through around looking for problems and solutions. I didn't realize that the church needed a complete overhaul of pretty much everything it had been doing. It was an aging church that had been declining for decades. I cannot tell you how many funerals I performed for the members of the church in just those first few years. They were in financial trouble too.

This church was wanting to get back to their glory days from roughly twenty years before my arrival. However, the community—and the world—had changed so drastically they would never again have the church they had in the 1980s. It is not so much they held on to the old traditional ways. It is they assumed the goal of a church is to have everyone happy. The reason "everyone was happy" in the 1980s is because they were effectively fulfilling what a church was supposed to be as they loved their community and shared Jesus with them. Somewhere they had lost vision and thought they could bring back the warmth and happy feelings and then people would start finding Jesus. They had lost their way.

I was ready to help them reach the neighborhood. I thought the phrase meant we would be a team that planned and executed together. They thought I would go get people from the neighborhood and teach them how to fit in at our church. I had no interest in making "church people" out of the neighbors. I wanted our neighborhood to meet Jesus. I presented this idea in a sermon series I preached to kick off the new year. I titled it "The Heart of Westside." In the heart of Westside were three things: share Jesus, show his love, and build believers. We all agreed those were great things. We didn't realize we had different definitions. I wanted those three items to drive everything at our church. The leadership wanted to make people happy, grow numerically, and not fight. So, everyone was unhappy, we didn't really grow numerically, and we fought. Also, we didn't share Jesus, show his love, or build believers.

During this time God blessed me with a mentor. He was a retired pastor with a lot of wisdom and patience. We would go out to eat and he would ask me all about the church, my philosophy on life, family, and more. In the three years we met together, the greatest lesson he taught me was a church could be one of two things. The church could be a machine or an oak tree. He encouraged me to pursue the oak tree church.

The machine church was one full of systems, numbers, and modern leadership principles. In the machine church the lead pastor was the CEO with all the answers. It was the lead pastor's will that would be done. He had the vision, and it was his job to lead everyone to accomplish it.

I think the machine church can work . . . sort of. I think the machine church can accomplish many of its goals if it has a five-talent lead pastor. I don't think there are many five-talent lead pastors. If you are reading this book, I'm sure you can name as many of them as I can. Those guys possess an amazing ability to attract people and influence people. I'm not a five-talent person. I tried it, and I don't have the skills to do it. There is a great chance you have failed at this too.

Let's embrace being two-talent servants. We won't travel the conference circuit selling books and captivating audiences. We will work in anonymity in old buildings that looked really cool in the 70s. We will step into broken situations and see the amazing healing of God played out on a life-changing, be it smaller, scale. Jesus didn't say we should try to be five-talent servants. Remember, they both heard the same things from the master.

The two-talent servant fits better in the oak tree church. The machine church that works will build great buildings, networks, colleges, and more. However, those churches don't seem to be able to stick around for more than one or two generations. The machine is built on the personality of its creator. There aren't machine churches in the New Testament. Well, there are, but they aren't treated too kindly in the book of Revelation. It's hard to make a case for a machine church from Paul's letters or Acts. There are more oak tree churches there.

The oak tree church isn't popular because it grows very slowly. An oak tree church can be any size. It just depends how long the oak tree church has been growing correctly. In the same way, most machine churches are probably small because you need a five-talent leader to make it work.

The oak tree church isn't built on processes or modern leadership principles. The oak tree church is one built on an understanding of church leadership from the Bible. The oak tree church looks to grow at a responsible rate through mundane things like one-on-one and tiny-group discipleship. The oak tree church doesn't have a discipleship process in and of itself. It has members who disciple. In the eight years I have lived in Florida, I have discipled guys two to three at a time. Each group gets one–two years of getting together weekly or every two weeks. Many of those people have become leaders in the church. More importantly, they have become better husbands, fathers, neighbors, and citizens. It takes tremendous time.

In the oak tree church, the lead pastor is always working himself out of a job.[20] He is looking to give away responsibility, authority, and influence. He isn't looking for the most awesome people. He is working with whomever God has brought to the church at the pace that person can go. It honors God, and it honors God's image bearers. The oak tree church doesn't have a five- or ten-year plan, it has a set of principles it functions from. For us, we exist to share Jesus, to show his love, and to build believers.

A loser can lead an oak tree church. A loser can also lead a machine church. A loser is the type of leader that God works best with anyway. A loser isn't sitting at the head of the table. A loser is the one who washes everyone else's feet. Jesus was a loser. Jesus chose to be a loser.[21] When none of the rest of the disciples would do it, Jesus stepped up, or rather kneeled down, to serve them in all by performing this menial task.

> When he had finished washing their feet, he put on his clothes and returned to his place. "Do you understand what I have done for you?" he asked them. "You call me 'Teacher' and 'Lord,' and rightly so, for that is what I am. Now that I, your Lord and Teacher, have washed your feet, you also should wash one another's feet. I have set you an example that you

should do as I have done for you. Very truly I tell you, no servant is greater than his master, nor is a messenger greater than the one who sent him. Now that you know these things, you will be blessed if you do them." (John 13:12–17)

Jesus has no fear of being a loser in the eyes of the world. He is teaching us our proper place in his kingdom. You and I are losers. We are not in charge. We are servants. We are blessed to be servants. We get to be servants. It should be an honor and a joy to be losers for the Lord. It is truly incredible that God stepped down on to the earth to serve his people. There is no other religion in the world that claims something like this. Why? Because they are all man-made. Only God could come up with something like this.

When I was at the little church in the little town and my dad asked me if I loved the people there, he might as well have asked if I was willing to wash their feet. I'm certain I wasn't. I'm thankful I am willing now. This is the attitude that helped me to be the leader who could help this church turn it all around and begin to reach people again: I ask him, "God am I a two-talent or a five-talent servant?" He answers, "Tim, that doesn't matter. Just start washing some feet."

After four years we had experienced a modest level of growth that got us noticed in a few church publications. However, we had never been less healthy. The bubbling conflict I started the chapter off with? Well, it was ready to bubble over.

CHAPTER 5

The Consultation

T hings were changing at our church, and it was getting rougher and rougher to be the lead pastor. We decided it was time to bring in some outside help for our leadership, so we hired a consultant. We picked this firm because it was the cheapest, and even then, we barely had enough money to pay for it.

We set up the first meeting, and the consultant wanted to speak with me individually. I'm pretty sure the first thing I told him was I didn't think I was lead pastor material. I couldn't handle the tensions between the staff, the elders, and the church members. I was pretty sure someone else could do all this far better than I could. I placed most of the blame on myself and my perceived lack of leadership skill. At this point I had been looking for teaching pastor jobs. I was confident in my preaching and teaching skills but felt incredibly inadequate at leading.

The consultant didn't agree with me at all. He told me in just the first few minutes that I was the right person for this job. Did I have flashbacks to the guy at camp when I was younger telling me I would accomplish something great? No. No, I didn't. I was certain I did not have what it took, and I was looking for people to agree so I wouldn't feel bad about leaving.

One constant in my life is that I tend to be a quitter, but God never gives me a way to quit. I have wanted to quit ministry several times but quickly found out that no one else wants me working in their field either! When God closed a door, he also closed the window, and the vents, and any other way I would have to flee. Maybe God made me a two-talent servant because if I had five talents, I wouldn't be working for him anymore.

The consultant gave us homework individually and as a team. He also had us assemble a group for the weekend he was going to come. We argued our way through it and completed everything. Then the weekend for him to come hit, and it was rough. One of our elders didn't show. Another elder only came to one day because, he said, being there both days was unfair to his family. The staff came ready to complain about, well, everything. I was embarrassed for the church members we had there to see the staff complain so much. I knew it reflected my lack of leadership follow-through.

Throughout the whole weekend the consultant looked to me to give the final answer on everything we talked about. That didn't make anyone happy! The consultant knew something we didn't. He saw we needed major changes within the group in the room. He knew I would have to do it. He knew I needed to consolidate power and then hand it out to new people.

Over the next two years almost everyone in that meeting left the church. The elders that had been there forever quit one by one. The staff moved on. Some of the church members left as well. It was the biggest turning point in our church. We were finally ready to become an oak tree church.

To become an oak tree church, I had to consolidate all the power. I had to make every decision. I had to lead every team. I had to make the coffee every Sunday morning (true story). Why? Because no one else did. Some saw my moves as a power grab. I saw them as a necessity. They were me fulfilling my role as the lowest servant in the church. I was finally using my two talents and working to make them two more for the glory of my master.

I knew doing things this way was unhealthy and unsustainable. It is great the lead pastor will make the coffee, but it is not good for the lead pastor to always make the coffee. I knew I needed to train leaders, but I didn't know how to train them or even what to train them to do. All I knew was the machine-church paradigm, and I didn't want to go through all this pain to start the stinking machine up all over again. I knew how I was going to fix it. Well, I prayed about it a lot and God gave me this idea. I'll open the church-leadership discussion to absolutely anyone in the church who wanted to talk about it.

I invited every single person in the church to meet with me on 10 Saturday mornings to read and discuss the book *When God Builds a Church* written by Bob Russell and Rusty Russell. About ten or twelve people consistently showed up to this group. None of the staff came. They didn't have any confidence in my leadership at that point. There are a variety of factors, but I won't get into them in this book.

This discussion group energized me, and I needed it. I could feel the burden of leadership move from my shoulders to the shoulders of other members of the church. We learned a lot, and we were even surprised with a visit from one of the authors of the book. It was a cool thing for our little church.

At the end of the ten weeks, we had identified four new elders to add to our team of two. These elders had a much different understanding of church and the role of a church leader. We spent most of our first year figuring out what a church elder is and what a church elder needs to do. We adopted a framework from another church and have been living by it ever since. We truly believe it is the framework from the Bible that shows us how to be an oak tree church. However, some tension remained within the church leadership. It was good because we needed to go all in on the oak tree and stop making any machine-church decisions.

This shift from machine to oak tree was also a shift for me. I was enamored with the machine church. I went to Bible college and got my start in ministry in the early 2000s, which means I was right there at the beginning of the numbers-at-all-costs movement of churches. We read the books and went to the conferences. I didn't care if the church was big. I cared if the church was growing quickly. If your church was growing quickly, you wrote a book and got all the cool speaking gigs at the best conferences. That's what I wanted, and it meant I would run a machine church. I really didn't have an idea of how to pastor an oak tree church. I knew it was a major shift. I also knew we were going to have to fumble through it and rely on God's provision and wisdom as we did.

The clearest example of this shift was when we needed to hire a new worship pastor. We had a guy filling in for a while. He started doing it because he was good at it, and he was the only person we thought could fill in to sing and lead a band at the last minute. He was well liked and doing a really good job. It was a huge blessing that none of us took for granted. However, he was not a pastor. He didn't go to Bible college. He didn't fit the mold. He was not an exciting hire. It has nothing to do with him personally. It is just we already knew him. He was not something fresh and new.

We knew we needed to hire someone to take the job full-time. This was a five-talent or two-talent servant question. Were we looking to hire someone who would be super awesome or someone who would be super faithful? You may think I'm going a bit too far. However, recently I came across a Facebook post from a church looking to hire someone and it read, "Are you awesome? We're hiring." Can you imagine Jesus using that line to pick out his disciples? This kind of thing just reinforces you must be awesome—or at least think of yourself as awesome—to succeed even in the church world. I feel like that church has missed the mark on staffing. We had to make sure that we didn't miss that mark. We needed to hire the right servant.

We did all of our previous hiring by conducting a national search and interviewing some people. We did it that way because we wanted the best available person. We wanted to hire all-stars, or rather, five-talent servants. It was the only way I had ever done hiring and the only way I had ever seen hiring done at a church. However, we were in a season of change. We pretty much had this blank slate to figure out who we were, and this was our first major decision.

Some of us started floating the idea of hiring our fill-in guy to go full-time. He was currently working another full-time job and doing this for us because he was a good guy. It certainly wasn't for the money. He had zero experience and no formal education for this role. However, his story was cool and indicative of what we wanted to be as a church. He was also very good at leading the band and singing. We could see he was doing well, and he was from the community our church is located in.

Do we offer the job to the two-talent guy or go digging for a five-talent servant? Did we know if he was a two-talent or five-talent guy? Lots of questions and lots of debating among the elders.

Why would we even consider hiring this guy with no experience and no education? Well, it felt like an oak tree church decision. He lived (and still lives) a few blocks from our church building. He was not a church guy. He was invited to come to church. He brought his wife and kids. They found Jesus here and gave their lives to him. They were baptized in our baptistry. They started serving right away. They were inviting people to church. Also, he had the talent to sing, play guitar, and was an exceptional leader. Maybe the better question would be, why wouldn't we hire this guy full-time? His story is exactly what we wanted to accomplish as a church. We wanted to reach non-Christians or unchurched people and see them become fully devoted followers of Jesus. This guy was the perfect example.

So, we hired the local guy. A few years later we have the healthiest band and tech team I've ever been around. He even volunteers in the middle school ministry. Let me repeat the previous statement with emphasis. He even VOLUNTEERS in the MIDDLE SCHOOL ministry! His wife oversees the tech, works with design, and is a fully engaged member of our community. My teenage son looks up to him as a mentor. They are active members of the church. Oh yah, and our worship is amazing. He doesn't just sing; he leads our church in worship. It is fun to see new people come to a worship service and be blown away at the quality of our band. He is excelling at our little church.

This decision to hire the local guy was not just a rational one. This decision was based in prayer and Bible study. We prayed and had a team praying for this decision. We looked through the New Testament to understand qualifications for pastors, elders, and leaders. We believed in the ministry of all believers. We knew I had the educational background to make sure our staff would stay on point. This was the defining moment of our becoming an oak tree church.

This decision gave us, and still gives us, confidence to continue to make oak tree church decisions. While many churches struggled through COVID and everything that came with it, we saw an increase in volunteer participation and financial giving. Our oak tree church is getting a little older and a little stronger. Those storms will come, but an oak tree is hard to knock over. A machine is always just one storm away from losing power.

CHAPTER 6

An Oak Tree Church

We are still discovering what an oak tree church is. Here is what we've discovered so far. An oak tree church grows very slowly. An oak tree church focuses on real-life leadership development. An oak tree church works with the people it has. An oak tree church is led by local elders, and elders serve the church in four specific ways. An oak tree church doesn't have campuses or a dream to build a larger building; it plants other churches.

An Oak Tree Church Grows Very Slowly

I started with this one because it is the hardest for me. I don't want growth to happen slowly, but I've learned I do want it to outlast me. I would rather have responsible growth than overnight "success." As much as I really do want our church to do well, I fight with feelings of inadequacy and discouragement. The slow growth of the oak tree church weighs the heaviest on me and has caused the most anxiety and doubt in my life. I wrote about this a few years ago, and it has remained my most read and shared blog post of all time[22].

Discouragement is a force in my life. Most of the time I feel it hanging over me, making me slouch in my chair. I can feel it in my stomach. It warms the back of my neck. It makes me feel so foolish. It really makes me embarrassed to be me.

Discouragement lies to me. It lies so well. It takes all the things I'm good at and makes me ashamed of them. If I'm great at meeting people—it makes me feel like a flake. If I come up with an amazing idea—it makes me feel like a loser who could never actually pull it off.

Discouragement yells at me to "shut up!" I have nothing important to say. Anything I would say would just come across as dreams of a man with his head in the clouds or empty platitudes by a pastor.

Discouragement tells me people can't really change. I am who I am, and it is all I will ever be. The man over there will never be any better off than he is right now, no matter what I might say, do, or pray.

I can never argue with discouragement either. He wins every single time. His comebacks are quicker than mine.

And his voice is so loud. It is so loud. It is louder than any other voice I've heard. I want to yell back at him, but I fear he is so often right.

Discouragement is an overbearing master who won't stop berating me. Even worse—he speaks through my thoughts directly into my mind. Worse yet—I wonder if I am the discouragement. Am I so stupid I'm doing this to myself?

When I am happy, discouragement is in the back of my mind. When I am celebrating, he comes to the party as a reminder I will never completely succeed. I will always fail even when I am succeeding.

Discouragement spends more time with me than my own wife and precious children. I know him better than I know anyone else. I hate him. I live in fear of him. Truth be said, he dictates much of what I do and what I say. Even when I fight him I can only do it for others. I can never fight him for my own cause. I hate him. I exhaust myself trying to defend or protect others from his rule. But I am completely powerless against him. He rules me.

When the Bible speaks of Satan as "The lion who stalks the earth looking for someone to devour," I know how he has devoured me. He has made me a slave to discouragement.

My only defense is to recognize that discouragement is lying to me. Jesus is the truth, and the truth will set me free. If discouragement is shouting in my ears, I must put Jesus' words directly in front of me. I must think about the words of Jesus. It is my only hope and the only possibility I have of not being a slave to discouragement.

Therefore, I read my Bible every morning. Therefore, I pray every morning. Therefore, I meet with a couple of Christian friends twice monthly. Therefore, I am open and honest with my wife and my family. Therefore, I am open and honest with the rest of our church staff and our elders. Because if I don't do these things—I stop seeing the truth of Jesus's power and I am, once again, crushed under the weight of discouragement.

I wonder how many other people have discouragement always hanging over their heads.

I know if you do, there is not very much I can write. I can write something that might make you feel a little better for a while. But if you are at all like me—discouragement is just sitting there waiting to pounce. I'd like to post a Bible verse to help you out. I can't do that. I have too much respect for discouragement's power. It is real.

To be honest, I'm writing this to deal with my own discouragement. I've found putting it out there helps me to see reality. If I let discouragement stay with me—I will be crushed. If I allow other people to see him—he shrinks back and disappears. He seems to be afraid of a group of people. Not all the time! No, he will run wild through a group of people. But he seems to get exposed as weakness when he hits a group of people who have studied Jesus.

This is unbelievable, even to me, but he is telling me not to post this. I will anyway.

Here is to us, if you know discouragement too. Let us lead a revolt against him. Let us expose who he really is—a lie.

Do you relate? I'll bet you do. There are two things in the past five years that have really helped me with this.

The first is counseling and medication. I won't spend too much time on this. I believe every person alive can benefit from Christian counseling. I have gone a few times. It has helped me to see more clearly. I don't think everyone needs medication. I did, and it changed my life. I was incredibly apprehensive about trying out medication for a lot of reasons. I wondered if it was a lack of faith in God or something equally as ridiculous. My wife convinced me to try it, and she was right.

The second is the knowledge we aren't responsible for numerical growth; we are responsible for faithful obedience. That's how the oak tree church grows. There is absolutely nothing flashy about obedience. You're probably not going to hear a speaker at a large church convention speaking on faithful obedience when things are hard. That topic will be covered at a minister's meeting with twenty or so in attendance. Obedience is rough. However, isn't that what we all want to hear? "Well done, good and faithful servant."

An Oak Tree Church Focuses on Real-Life Leadership Development

This is not a leadership book. I think I've read a hundred books on the topic. They are all insightful to the situation they address. No one has written a book about how to do leadership development at my church. (Would be nice, right?!). Also, I know the Bible is the book for leadership development in a church—thanks. However, if a book could do effective leadership development at my church, there wouldn't be a need for me, and there wouldn't be work for our already developed leaders to do.

Like everything else in an oak tree church, leadership development moves slowly. We don't have a formal discipleship process. We have a general idea of how someone can move from seeker to fully devoted follower of Christ. We have an idea that leaders of the church should be developing newer leaders of the church. We talk about it, and we encourage each other to be discipling. We keep each other accountable on this. We check in on each other. We value this.

I don't visit everyone in our church in their homes. I don't do many home visits at all. However, I have never turned down someone's request to visit them in their home. I focus my time on a few people at a time. It's not that I don't care about others. It's not that I don't pray or counsel. It's not that I'm unavailable. It is that I understand leadership development to be very time heavy, and I don't have the capacity to develop every person in our church family. I have a few people I work with for a year or two at a time. These people become solid leaders. They lead not only in our church but in their families and in our community. They are oak tree people.

Something else makes this very slow. Once we develop church leaders, some of them move on to serve in other churches. It is great for the kingdom, and an oak tree church celebrates that. Our healthy little oak tree church can help other churches become healthy as well. It is awesome.

An Oak Tree Church Works with the People It Has

We recognize every person in our church is there because God placed him or her in this church at this time. This church isn't my church. This church isn't his or her church. This is God's church, and we are fortunate to be a part of it. That means every person here is just as valuable as everyone else.

An oak tree church is anchored in principles but driven by the gifts, talents, and interests of its people. As I've stated before, our church exists to share Jesus, show his love, and build believers. Those are our principles, and they can be expressed in myriad ways. For instance, in our little church we have an abnormally high percentage of kids with autism. This didn't happen because we formed a team to reach autistic kids. It happened because we had a family who had an autistic child we worked with to incorporate into our student programming. This led to another family finding our church for a place for their child to fit in. In this way, the ministry and reach of the church isn't limited to the vision of one person or group of people. The entire church family is involved in ministry.

We don't wait to get the "right people." We don't have a secret list of people in the congregation with stats on their giving, atten-dance, and perceived skills (yes, this is a real thing happening at some churches). Jesus picked a bunch of normal people. I use the phrase to refer to the disciples he picked. I also use the phrase to refer to our church. I also use the phrase to refer to you and me. We are a bunch of normal people Jesus has picked. We aren't nec-essarily the "right people" by human standards.

An Oak Tree Church Is Led by Elders Who Serve in Four Specific Ways

The journey to this realization was fun. We had just completed reading the book with anyone who wanted to be there. We had just decided who we think would be good elders and who meet the biblical quali-fications of an elder. We asked them and they said yes. We presented them to the church, and it was unanimous. I was also made an elder. So, we now have elders. The first order of business? Figure out what we are supposed to be doing. We all had previous church leadership experiences; some were good, and some were bad. We took bits and pieces, but we all felt incomplete. So, we decided to search the Bible and look to what other churches are doing. Then we found it.

One of us found a free document[23] from an organization called E2 Effective Elders.[24] This document went through the Bible and made a clear case for what elders are supposed to be doing. Elders are to shepherd the congregation, oversee the ministry of prayer, over-see the ministry of the Word, and set polity. Those four areas have become the areas we talk through in our monthly elders' meetings. We do our best to stick to those four areas and not micromanage the staff or other church leaders. We want our leaders to have the support to lead their teams. We realize this happens when we stick to these four vitally important areas.

The document is free for anyone and explains all of this very well. Quickly, shepherding the congregation is making sure all members are cared for, loved well, inspired to growth, and not alone. The ministries of prayer and the Word are to make sure our church is a praying church and a church of the Bible. Lastly, we set polity. Polity is giving our leaders a clear picture of success and the parameters they need to stay inside to accomplish it.

An Oak Tree Church Plants Other Churches

An oak tree church doesn't have campuses. We believe in the ministry of all believers. Let me use the following as an example.

I believe a biblical message preached by a person you know is of far more value than a biblical message from someone you don't know. The message can't be separated from the person. I can't be inspired by a message about loving my spouse by a guy who tears his wife down. I am far more inspired by simply watching a guy support his wife's dreams than listening to anything he says. An oak tree church may not have a spectacular sermon every week, but it gives voice to those who live a spectacular life. In conversation with a pastor who has had much numerical growth in his churches, he said, "My youth pastor from when I was growing up is the person I know who is most like Jesus. However, he was not very good at his job." I heard it a couple decades ago, and it makes less sense now than it did then. Didn't the apostle Paul say something like "follow me as I follow Jesus?" I don't remember reading about attendance matrixes.

This principal carries on through the rest of the church. A local pastor with local elders and local members is the best way for a church to be a church. It is playing the long game. It is being an oak tree church.

We don't have campuses and we don't plan to have campuses. We aren't interested in reproducing our church. Our church is particular to the place it is. We are interested in helping new communities get their New Testament church. I don't remember reading about "The Church of Philippi—Jerusalem Campus."

CHAPTER 7

Hearing the Same Thing

I believe the greatest opening line of any book ever written was penned by a certified five-talent servant, Rick Warren.[25] In his book *The Purpose Driven Life*, he writes, "It is not about you." I am thinking of using this phrase every time I teach anything from the Bible. Pray first and then have everyone repeat this phrase. This has been my problem many times. This may have something to do with our current religious movement of making everything about ourselves. I doubt many first-century Christians chose a church because of what it had to offer them. They didn't care about the coffee, the parking lot, or the service times. Did any first-century Christians actually "choose" a church?

"Where do you go?"

"Oh, I go to the only church in the city."

"No way! Me too!"

Little known fact, but the first city to have two Christian churches in it was in Jerusalem. The reason the second church started? Worship styles.[26]

I look at Jesus's parable, and I wonder where I fit in. Now that we are halfway through the book, let's go ahead and move this from egocentric to Christocentric. Don't get mad at me. We had to start with ourselves to realize how short we fall. The next thing we need to notice about this parable is that Jesus didn't use it to explain "me." This parable isn't meant to explain Tim Boyd[27] and all his intricacies. No, I am in the audience. I am not learning about me. I'm learning about the nature of God and the kingdom of God. What do I learn from this parable? I learn it is the master who gives out the talents and it is the master who checks back on their use. They are also the master's talents. He entrusts his servants with them; he doesn't just give them away.

First, it's the master who gives out the talents and who checks back on the use of the talents. Matthew 25:19 reads, "Now after a long time the master of those servants came and settled accounts with them." In the parable's timeline, we are currently in the space between verses 18 and 19. The master has given us something. The master is coming back to settle accounts. He doesn't care if you have produced five, two, or one more talent. He does want you to produce something. If you just hand back what he gave you, you lose. Possibly the only way to be a loser is to do absolutely nothing with what the master has given you.

Second, they are the master's talents, not the servants' talents. The servants were entrusted with this amount of money, and they were supposed to do something with it. We understand this as stewardship. We don't own anything; rather, we are stewards. This started in the garden of Eden when Adam was told to care for the garden. This included enjoying the fruits of the garden.[28] Stewarding God's resources should be fun. Sin makes it hard. After the fall, Adam still had to take care of the ground, but now it wasn't the original garden and there would be weeds and back-breaking work to enjoy those fruits. I remember something my wife said once when we got a really big repair bill that we could barely afford. I was all bent out of shape and pouting about it. She just said, "Well it's God's money, and if he wants to waste it on that, it's his business." I didn't get into the theology of the matter; I just enjoyed the attitude behind the words. She understood the first rule of stewardship—it's not yours.

Third, two of them heard the exact same thing from the master. It didn't matter how many talents they had. Both got to hear, "Well done, good and faithful servant! You have been faithful with a few things; I will put you in charge of many things. Come and share your master's happiness!" (Matthew 25:21, 23)

Well done.

It is not what I want to hear from the guy grilling my steak, but it is what I want to hear from the master.[29]

This phrase is what I've been looking for my entire life. I just want to be told I'm doing well with the things I'm supposed to be doing well with. I want to hear from the only person who really knows what it means to live life well. I want to know from the Creator and Sustainer of life I've done well with what I've been given. It is not even that I *want* to hear it from God; it is that I *must* hear it from God. I have heard that encouraging phrase from many people, and it isn't enough to satisfying my desire completely. I need to hear it from God. My soul yearns to hear this from God. I can doubt someone else's motives or reasons or even capacity to encourage me. I can't doubt God's. He is perfect and his praise is perfect. If he chooses to tell me, "Well done," then I know beyond a shadow of a doubt I have done well.

The master has been clear with how I can be in a position to hear "well done." We've already looked at in this book. It is about faithful obedience. Think about the parable of the sheep and the goats (Matthew 25:31–46). Why did the sheep hear something good, and the goats hear something bad? The sheep's actions showed they were living in faithful obedience. The sheep were the people who had done something. Their faith was living and active. Their deeds showed their faith. The goats' actions showed they had buried their talent in the ground. The goats didn't do the things they knew were good. They thought they would do them, but they never actually did them. They were not faithful or obedient. They did not do things well. They only thing they deserved was what they got—punishment. James tackles this in James 2:14–19

What good is it, my brothers and sisters, if someone claims to have faith but has no deeds? Can such faith save them? Suppose a brother or a sister is without clothes and daily food. If one of you says to them, "Go in peace; keep warm and well fed," but does nothing about their physical needs, what good is it? In the same way, faith by itself if it is not accompanied by action, is dead. But someone will say, "You have faith; I have deeds." Show me your faith without deeds, and I will show you my faith by my deeds. You believe that there is one God. Good! Even the demons believe that—and shudder."

We aren't going to hear "well done" simply by having good intentions. "Well done" is reserved for someone who has done something well. We show our faith by our deeds. Then we do our best not to post those deeds on social media. Perhaps the more that we hear "well done" in this world, the less chance we are to hear it from God.

Faithful obedience is to make sure I am ready and willing to hear the Spirit of God and obey his voice. I think of Joseph from the Christmas story. His faithful obedience is remarkable. He was already a good man. He faced a terrible situation in that the woman he was betrothed to had become pregnant. He had figured out what he was going to do, which was to put her aside quietly as not to embarrass her. He was going to be a good man and follow God while also not hurting Mary. As a friend, it would have been hard for me to disagree with anything he was thinking. His determination seemed fair and compassionate. Then God told him to do something different—marry her anyway. Joseph woke up and obeyed what God had said, not what Joseph was thinking. In the Scripture it looks like he had this dream from God and then the very next day followed through on it. He took no time to mull it over or talk with friends. He just got up and did it. That's miraculous and a testimony to Joseph's faithful obedience. This often gets lost in the Christmas story. Why? Well, the story isn't about Joseph; it's about Jesus. I'm not Jesus, nor will I ever be. But I can relate to Joseph. I am not divine. I can, however, hear from God and change my action based on his leading and teaching. It is the position I pray I am in at all times. It's the faithful obedience that I need to be expressing.

"You have been faithful with a few things."

This is the sum of what I need to do with my life. People may ask, "What's God's will for my life?" Well, here it is. You need to be faithful with what the master has given you. The meaning of life is here in this parable. When I became a Christian, I took the position of servant of the master. The master has entrusted me with his talent. It is my duty to serve my master and use the talent he has entrusted to me. I am to be faithful with what he has given to me. This must take precedence over everything else in my life. This is why I pray Jesus's simple prayer every morning. The Lord's Prayer goes like this, "Our Father, who art in heaven, hallowed be thy name; thy kingdom come; thy will be done on earth as it is in heaven. Give us this day our daily bread; and forgive us our trespasses as we forgive those who trespass against us; and lead us not into temptation but deliver us from evil. Amen." This parable finds itself in this prayer. It is not mine—it is yours. Please help me use it. Please forgive me when I don't. Then I add, "please help me be the best servant, husband, father, friend, and pastor I can be today." Those are the primary areas of my life, and I need to be faithfully obedient in each of them in that order.

When it comes to the church, I want the master to see a strong oak tree that outlives me and provides for generations to come. I don't want the master to see I have built something for me or my name or my legacy. Those are easy things to write. Those are incredibly hard things to live every single day. Weekly I will have decisions about what type of church I am going to work at. Those little decisions add up over time and steer the direction of the church.

I don't want to be faithful with a few things. I want to be faithful with a bunch of awesome and envy-producing things. I wasn't called to live that way, and it is not healthy for me. I'm living my best life when I'm right there in the will of God faithfully obeying him. If he wants me faithful with a few things, then that is what must be best for me.

"I will put you in charge of many things."

I'm not sure what he means by this. (I told you I was only a two-talent servant.). I don't know if it means in this life or in heaven. I don't care. Well, that's not true. My flesh wants to be put in charge of more things on this earth. I want more recognition. I want my shoes on Preachers N Sneakers.[30] However, I have relented, and I don't need to know what this means. If this is what God is calling me to, then he will equip me for it as long as I'm obedient.

I only need to focus on being faithful with a few things. Why? Because he finishes with this.

"Come and share My happiness!"

So, I can share in my master's happiness! This is the payoff I'm looking for. I assume this is eternal heaven, the place that Christians believe is the eternal rest. It's the very real place where we will be with Jesus for all eternity in the house that he is building for us. There will be no mourning, crying, pain or death. We will be made completely whole. There is no sin and therefore no effect of sin. Everything there is just as it should be. It is perfect, and it is better than we can comprehend. It is the perfect and eternal with the perfect and eternal one. This is what awaits me. This is why I'm faithful. This is why I can't choose the fleshy route of building my kingdom, making my name great, or rushing the church to be something it shouldn't be.

This should be enough for me. This should be enough for you. If the promise of heaven is not enough, we have a problem that needs to be addressed. The problem is most likely pride. I'll write this a different way. If I don't regard heaven as the greatest reward and completely worth giving my life away for, then I don't quite get Christianity. If being with God alive forever in heaven isn't what we desire most, what else would it be? What have we put in place of that great reward? Jesus's words, "Where your treasure is, there your heart will be also" (Matthew 6:21), ring true in this assessment. What is the greatest thing you can think of happening to you? Anything less than heaven will reveal what's wrong in your heart. I've heard people talking about different sized mansions in heaven. I always respond, "When I get to heaven, I think I'm just going to fall on the ground and yell out 'Oh my goodness! I'm in heaven!'"

We cannot forget there were three servants. The other servant did not hear these words. He went out and buried his talent. This servant heard, "You wicked, lazy servant! So, you knew I harvest where I have not sown and gather where I have not scattered seed? Well then, you should have put my money on deposit with the bankers, so when I returned I would have received it back with interest. So take the bag of gold from him and give it to the one who has ten bags. For whoever has will be given more, and they will have an abundance. Whoever does not have, even what they have will be taken from them. And throw that worthless servant outside, into the darkness, where there will be weeping and gnashing of teeth." The master has much more to say this servant, and it's terrible.

He was afraid so he did nothing. I feel this one in my bones. I have wanted to quit the ministry several times. I've already shared that no one else wants to hire me! One day I was in Sam's Club doing the math on how many vending machines I would need to have to replace my church income.[31] It has been rough at times. I've wanted to hide the talent in the ground, but God has continued to give me opportunities to use it instead. God is good. God is also patient.

I see this parable as showing us the servant who didn't faithfully obey the master was tossed into hell. I've also already admitted I'm only a two-talent servant. Another certified five-talent servant, Warren Wiersbe, writes, "It is dangerous to build theology on parables, for parables illustrate truth in vivid ways. The man was dealt with by the Lord, he lost his opportunity for service, and he gained no praise or reward. To me, that is outer darkness."[32] First, let me state clearly that I believe in an eternal hell. Now, let me state hell isn't the only bad thing can happen to a person. It is the worst, but not the only, bad thing. How many people struggle with identity and purpose because they haven't been using their talent for the master? Can I be so bold as to say every person alive feels this way *unless* they are using their talent for the master? Because it is exactly what I think. I think we all need to live like losers.

CHAPTER 8

Living Like a Loser ... for the Lord

One of the most freeing thoughts in my life was when I finally realized I was a loser. I was not a loser to many others. I was a loser to what my younger self thought I should be. I didn't live up to the potential I saw in myself. Ha! Today I completely embrace the title of loser, and I love it. It helps me with my pride. It helps me be easier on myself. It helps me recognize I need God for pretty much everything. It helps me enjoy my life.

When it comes to feeling like a loser, I know I'm not alone. Here is list of just terrible thoughts you might have about yourself.

You should have been further along than you are at your age.

You need to make a name for yourself.

Is this really the life you wanted to provide for your family?

You should be putting more into retirement.

You should have more in retirement.

Other people are doing better than you are.

She is younger and she is your boss.

Thought you would have moved by now.

You still haven't started that business.

You never did make that million.

You've been in your starter home quite a while.

Second marriage?

You used to be pretty.

Whole thing never really took off, did it?

There are so many more, and it comes down to this: we all have unfulfilled dreams. We all feel like there are other people who have it better together than we do. We all have something we feel insecure about. We are all unsuccessful. We are all losers.

Chasing success will leave us devastated and empty. Worldly success is impossible to achieve because the line is always moving. Chasing worldly success always results in pain.

The success line is always moving! You can never catch it. No matter how well you are doing, someone else is always doing better. Don't believe me! What about the billionaire's race to space? Look at this article about Jeff Bezos, a person many believe has achieved quite of bit of success.

> Space travel, he said, in a hype video posted to Instagram,[33] was the thing he'd wanted to do all his life. Bezos didn't seem to be exaggerating. "I am really interested in space exploration, but the truth is, it is some number of years off," he told an Amazon employee, back in 1996. Selling books online, Bezos said, was something "to do in the meantime." The meantime took longer than Bezos had hoped. He created Blue Origin in 2000, before Elon Musk had SpaceX or Richard Branson had Virgin Galactic. But Branson beat him by first putting an astronaut into space, in 2018; Musk beat him by first putting a rocket into orbit, in 2010; and Musk, the recipient of a giant NASA contract to build a lunar lander, will likely beat him to the moon. Bezos is eager to steal a win from his rivals. The announcement of his coming mission, on July 20th, coinciding with the anniversary of the Apollo moon landing, would do just that. Bezos would achieve something neither Branson nor Musk has yet done: he would put *himself* into space."[34]

Branson beat him by nine days. How bad did that feel? I once had a school record broken the very next year. That one still stings!

We even move the line ourselves. I bought a sixty-five-inch TV, and it was amazing. Until my friend got a seventy-five-inch TV. Now it feels like I can't even see the football when I'm watching my tiny sixty-five-inch screen. Maybe you buy the house of your dreams, and in a few years your dreams grow. Solomon experienced this and wrote about it.

> The words of the Teacher, son of David, king in Jerusalem: "Meaningless! Meaningless!" says the Teacher. "Utterly meaningless! Everything is meaningless." What do people gain from all their labors at which they toil under the sun?

This is the question. Right there. Don't you love Scripture that seems to need no commentary or explanation? It seems like Solomon was living right in our neighborhood.

> Generations come and generations go, but the earth remains forever. The sun rises and the sun sets and hurries back to where it rises. The wind blows to the south and turns to the north; round and round it goes, ever returning on its course.

Things will keep on happening. You don't have the impact you think you have.

> All streams flow into the sea, yet the sea is never full. To the place the streams come from, there they return again. The eye never has enough of seeing, nor the ear it is fill of hearing.

Did this guy have a smartphone? Seriously. If this isn't prophecy—what is? BTW—to me this proves the Bible is written by God because he knows us at our core.

> What has been will be again, what has been done will be done again; there is nothing new under the sun. Is there anything of which one can say, "Look! This is something new"? It was here already, long ago; it was here before our time. No

one remembers the former generations, and even those yet to come will not be remembered by those who follow them. (Ecclesiastes 1:1–11)

Solomon, the guy who wrote this, had more wisdom, money, and power than any of us could ever dream of. He was not a five-talent servant. He was a million-talent servant.

I think this Scripture gives us the definitive answer: there is no way to achieve worldly success. We will always want more. The line is moving, and you will never catch it. Of course, Jesus speaks about this too: "What good is it for someone to gain the whole world, yet forfeit their soul?" How many stories have you heard of people chasing their dreams and losing their families? Twenty years ago I wanted to be Tiger Woods, but I am certainly happy it never happened. That's not to downplay the recent reports of him doing much better with life now. I'm pointing out that I'm glad I didn't have to face the temptations on the level that he did. I am still enjoying the original story of my life, and it hasn't had to drastically change because of huge public mistakes. Would I rather have a healthy and happy family or achieve worldly success? How many stories have you heard of people realizing their dreams and then realizing their dreams weren't enough?

What is worldly success to God? In a word: failure. To achieve success by the world's standards is to fail by God's standards. A couple of Old Testament stories illustrate this well.

First is the tower of Babel in Genesis 11. God told humans to spread out over the face of the earth and populate it. He clearly defined what success was for them. They simply needed to listen to him and then obey what he said. However, they wanted to do something great for themselves and build a city with a tower reaching to the heavens (something that still impresses us). They had their dreams and their definition of success, and it was not what God had for them. Does this sound familiar? Thankfully, we don't know what the cost of them completing the project would be to us now. How much different would life be if God hadn't intervened and enforced his well? In his great grace, God scattered them anyway. Why? He has a plan. His plan is right. We can assume his plan is also good for us. God's plan happens when we obey him, and when we don't, as the author just demonstrated in the Babel narrative.

God's idea of success and man's idea of success is on display in the first king of Israel. The people wanted an earthly king. It was not good enough for them to have God as their king. They wanted to be successful as defined by the nations surrounding them. So, God chose for them the most successful-looking guy in their nation. We learn a few things about Saul right away. He is tall and handsome. Look at the leaders and middle-management types in the world still today—for the most part they are tall and handsome. Sports talk radio host Colin Cowherd has an interesting theory on "quarter-back face."[35] He states the better-looking young men are picked to be quarterbacks when they are younger. The poor Israelites didn't realize they were already being led by a five-talent leader. Well, more than that, but you get what I mean. They instead petitioned God for the one-talent servant, the guy who was full of fear.

Saul lives up to his worldly success, that is, he is a huge failure who is full of fear and ends up really hurting the people he should be caring for. In one story God tells King Saul to go the Amalekites and kill everything, including the livestock. Saul kept the good live-stock. The story is in 1 Samuel 15:12–23.

> Early in the morning Samuel got up and went to meet Saul, but he was told, "Saul has gone to Carmel. There he has set up a monument in his own honor and has turned and gone on down to Gilgal."
>
> When Samuel reached him, Saul said, "The Lord bless you! I have carried out the Lord's instructions." But Samuel said, "What then is this bleating of sheep in my ears? What is this lowing of cattle I hear?"

Samuel has caught Saul. First, Saul is building a monument to himself. I've been there. I've never had the resources to build a physical monument, but I've certainly taken the time to steer conversations to look at me as a monumentally successful guy. Now with social media, it is even easier to build such monuments. We can all build our own and get our own group of followers and fans.

> Saul answered, "The soldiers brought them from the Amalekites; they spared the best of the sheep and cattle to sacrifice to the Lord your God, but we totally destroyed the rest."

C'mon, man. Saul is an impressive fearful leader. He pulls off some great deflecting here in just one sentence. He blames someone else, tries to flatter his accuser, and then states he still really did complete the mission. To quote Ron Burgundy, "I'm not even mad. I'm impressed." Worse yet, I'm guilty. I can do this too. It is bad when I do this with people. It is terrible when I do this with God. It is sinister when I do this with myself. I try to convince myself I'm doing God's will and getting worldly success too. It doesn't happen. It can't happen. In Matthew 5:11 Jesus states, "Blessed are you when people insult you, persecute you and falsely say all kinds of evil against you because of me." Doesn't feel too successful.

> "Enough!" Samuel said to Saul. "Let me tell you what the Lord said to me last night."
> "Tell me," Saul replied.
> Samuel said, "Although you were once small in your own eyes, did you not become the head of the tribes of Israel? The Lord anointed you king over Israel. And he sent you on a mission, saying, 'Go and completely destroy those wicked people, the Amalekites; wage war against them until you have wiped them out.' Why did you not obey the Lord? Why did you pounce on the plunder and do evil in the eyes of the Lord?"

"But I did obey the Lord," Saul said. "I went on the mission the Lord assigned me. I completely destroyed the Amalekites and brought back Agag their king.

Saul tells Samuel he completed the mission *and* achieved success by the standard of the neighboring nations. This is the same lie I pursue. I want worldly success and for God to tell me, "Well done good and faithful servant." I have to fight this with regular Bible study, prayer, and continually opening up to friends and family. I can't fight this lie alone. I need the camaraderie of others who are also trying to be obedient servants.

"The soldiers took sheep and cattle from the plunder, the best of what was devoted to God, in order to sacrifice them to the Lord your God at Gilgal."
But Samuel replied: "Does the Lord delight in burnt offerings and sacrifices as much as in obeying the Lord? To obey is better than sacrifice, and to heed is better than the fat of rams. For rebellion is like the sin of divination, and arrogance like the evil of idolatry. Because you have rejected the word of the Lord, he has rejected you as king."

Saul sure thought he was successful. But he didn't obey God, so God took away the "success" he had handed to him.
Think of the Laodicean church in Revelation 3:17: "You say, 'I am rich; I have acquired wealth and do not need a thing.' But you do not realize you are wretched, pitiful, poor, blind and naked." Translation: "your awesome success means nothing to God—to God you look like someone who can't even take care of themselves." This is exactly how I felt. I was something. I was full of potential. I was awesome. God looked at me and said, "Tim, you aren't ready. You're too full of yourself to have any part of me. Come to me and I will give you want you need to do the work I have for you to do."

If success doesn't come from human achievement, where does it come from? I believe all the worldly definitions of success are by-products of something else. The world defines success as having accomplished enough that I can be happy and peaceful. Happiness and peace, or rather "contentment," comes only from God. We get it through our humble obedience to him. It is free. This is the "success" killer. Why do we care so much about being successful? Because we believe the lie achieving our definition of success will bring us the happiness and peace we want, when, in reality, God gives those to you when you humbly obey him.

The worldly hear and assume you must lose to follow God. Then you remain a loser who doesn't get to have ambition, goals, fun, desires, and the like. The reality is the worldly will work to gain the whole world (an impossibility) and will lose their own souls. The godly give their souls to God and God gives them the whole world and heaven for all eternity.

Jesus is the ultimate winner full of joy and peace. We read that in the "Christ Hymn" in the book of Philippians.

> Who, being in very natureGod, did not consider equality with God something to be used to his own advantage; rather, he made himself nothing by taking the very nature of a servant, being made in human likeness. And being found in appearance as a man, he humbled himself by becoming obedient to death— even death on a cross! Therefore, God exalted him to the highest place and gave him the name that is above every name, that at the name of Jesus every knee should bow, in heaven and on earth and under the earth, and every tongue acknowledge Jesus Christ is Lord, to the glory of God the Father. (Philippians 2:6–11)

Jesus models what it means to be a loser for God. What does it net him? He was exalted to the highest place. Jesus says in Mathew 10:39, "Whoever finds their life will lose it, and whoever loses their life for my sake will find it." I had heard this verse before. Even during my fame-seeking twenties I knew this verse. I taught it. I guess I didn't understand it yet. I was trying to live up to *my* potential. It was all about me. If the master had handed me a thousand talents, I would have used them all to build my brand. It was out of God's great grace he handed me two talents. It was out of God's great mercy he helped me get into a position to use them. He helped me lose my life. He truly answered the "stick" prayer I prayed around that campfire in northern Minnesota.

I relate to Saul. Well, I'm not tall and handsome or a king, but I am filled with anxiety and doubt. So, the prophet's words to Saul help me out. God desires obedience, not sacrifices. He wants you to listen to him more than he wants you to lead a megachurch. The second King of Israel knew this well. David wrote this:

> You do not delight in sacrifice, or I would bring it; you do not take pleasure in burnt offerings. My sacrifice, O God, is a broken spirit; a broken and contrite heart you, God, will not despise. (Psalm 51:16–17)

David knew from his own experience of failure that success to God can look like penitence. Penitence—the action of feeling or showing sorrow and regret for having done wrong[36]. Repentance. Do you feel like a loser because you have done something bad? God is looking for you to come to him and tell him you're sorry and would like to do better. That is success.

Success comes from obedience and knowing God. We know God through his Word. Joshua 1:8 says, "Keep this Book of the Law always on your lips; meditate on it day and night, so you may be careful to do everything written in it. Then you will be prosperous and successful." Reading the Bible leads to success? Just think of all the things you have done, spent time on, and spent money on that haven't brought you the success you were looking for. Can it be as simple as reading the Bible? Yes.

Let us embrace being "losers in this world." It is the key. I can't live up to the world's definition of success because it keeps changing. It is unattainable. I can't live up to my own definition of success because my ambition, insecurity, nostalgia, etc. lie to me. I can't live up to your definition of success because you keep changing your mind too.

I can, however, live up to God's definition of success because he helps me attain it.

CHAPTER 9

All Your Meaningless Days

The greatest case study in chasing worldly success is Solomon, the wisest person to ever live according to Scripture. With his extreme wisdom came wealth, power, pleasure, status, prestige, and more. He might have been the fabled ten-talent servant. In his book of Ecclesiastes, he starts with his thesis that everything under the sun is meaningless, a chasing after the wind. He makes this point poetically in chapter 1. Then, basically, the next eight chapters of his book focus on his chase of success in all the ways the world has to offer success. I'll take some leaps, but I'll say he went further down each of those paths than anyone ever else had. For instance, one thousand women were his to sleep with. He had wealth beyond compare, and it was not tied to shareholder value. He built amazing structures. People came from all over to fawn over his speaking and what he had built all around him. Solomon had the wisdom to analyze everything he was doing, and at the same time, he had the wealth to do anything that a person could do on earth. At the end of the searches, he found nothing of value. This is an incredible place for him to end up. Shouldn't all of us stop trying to pursue success in any of the ways that he did? It's like when the waiter warns you that the plate is hot, but you touch it anyway. You know the waiter has no reason to lie to you, but you just can't help trying it. Solomon does it all and ends up realizing it was meaningless. Then he wrote this:

Go, eat your food with gladness, and drink your wine with a joyful heart, for God has already approved what you do. Always be clothed in white, and always anoint your head with oil. Enjoy life with your wife, whom you love, all the days of this meaningless life God has given you under the sun—all your meaningless days. For this is your lot in life and in your toilsome labor under the sun. Whatever your hand finds to do, do it with all your might, for in the realm of the dead, where you are going, there is neither working nor planning nor knowledge nor wisdom. (Ecclesiastes 9:7–10)

What is success? Solomon seems to say it can be counted in four ways with a twist. The twist is the four ways don't work unless we have repented and are under the Lordship of Jesus. These work only when we are in God's kingdom. If we are in God's kingdom and faithfully following him and ready to hear from him, then there are four markers of success.

First, he states, "eat your food with gladness and drink your wine with a joyful heart." He is talking about enjoying the beautifully small and mundane things on earth. God has already given us enough to have joy and gladness. It is all right here. It's always been here. He created it for us. We get a sunrise and a sunset every single day. We get the night sky, the rolling plains of the prairie, the sound of waves crashing on the beach, and the feel of the crisp mountain air rolling up the path. Just think of all the ways we can eat meat—grilled, smoked, baked, boiled, fried, sous vide. That's not even to mentions all the different types of meats, cuts of meat, and flavors of meat.[37] For many of us, it gets downright embarrassing how much we enjoy our morning coffee. There are so many gifts God gives us that are so incredibly mundane. The billionaires can race to space while the rest of us can look up to it for free. Not long ago I was lying on our trampoline with a few of my kids staring up at the night sky. Even though we live in an urban area, the stars were really popping that night. To our surprise and joy, we got to see a shooting star. My son asked, "Dad, did God do that just for us?" I had to answer with a yes. God did that for us. God made this for us. God gave me you. God gave you me. God gave us the gift of being alive and together in this moment. Success is taking so much delight in God we can't help but delight in his gifts all around us. I'm certain that us losers are just so happy with what God has done for us that we miss out on some great side hustles, gigs, and other ways to capitalize on our perceived talent. Who worried more about using their talent? Was it the two-talent or five-talent servant? Or was it the one-talent servant? I'm convinced it was the one-talent servant. The others were too busy using what the master had given them.

Some of us feel like losers because we fear that we are wasting our lives. I will continue to contend that the two-talent and five-talent servants didn't worry about that. It was the one-talent servant who lived in fear. I lived in this fear of wasting my life. I didn't realize that God had had me where he wanted me for a specific reason and specific season. Solomon pursued everything and found no purpose or meaning. In fact, Solomon's conclusion to pursuing all earthly success and not "wasting his life"? It was to say that it's all meaningless. When you and I are saved by Jesus and in the will of our Father, we can eat and drink and be merry and live the gift of life to the fullest.

Second, "always be clothed in white and always anoint your head with oil." This is what they would do for celebrations. It was the opposite of what you would wear in mourning. God encourages us to be happy. It is okay to smile and laugh. It is okay to be happy. In fact, it is good to be content. One of the defining characteristics of a follower of Jesus is inner contentment unshakeable by outside circumstances. Paul writes in Philippians 4:11, "Not that I am speaking of being in need, for I have learned in whatever situation I am to be content." Every day is a celebration for the servant of the master. Remember, he gave the servants $21 million, $42 million, and over $100 million. They each were given what we would all consider a great sum of money. Honestly, if you are reading a book titled "Loser," then I assume you don't even have $21 million. That would put you in the same boat as me.[38] In the parable, the master gave each servant an awesome amount of money. He gave each of us the gift of life. He has given us the gift of love. He has given us his Son Jesus who died on the cross so you and I can be saved through him. We are, literally, on our way to heaven. These are all reasons to celebrate like we won the lottery.

Do you know how to celebrate? My wife does. When my wife celebrates her birthday, we celebrate for the entire month. It is not an option. It is a way of life. Once the calendar turns from June to July, she lets us all know it is her birth month. Her birthday is on the 26th, so it really lasts about an entire month. This is the way to look at life as a Christian. When we are saved, the calendar has flipped from June to July. The rest of our days on earth are just a celebration until we hit the big celebration on the 26th!

Third, we are to enjoy life with our spouse. I don't think we all have to be married. Paul writes about this a little in his first letter to the Corinthians. I think this means if you are married or get married, you should see this as a way for both of you to enjoy your lives together. There are over fifteen trillion books[39] written on the topic of Christian date nights, so I don't think I need to go further with that topic. However, it is odd Solomon wrote this. He famously had seven hundred wives.[40] It doesn't seem like he practiced what he preached. Ultimately, his many wives led him astray and he lost God's blessing. Knowing something doesn't mean you are doing something. It was not their fault. Solomon's problem was Solomon. He let himself be led astray. That doesn't mean his words weren't inspired by God. If we only had the words written by those who didn't sin, we would only have the words of Jesus.

Interestingly enough, Solomon also wrote this: "Let your fountain be blessed, and rejoice in the wife of your youth, a lovely deer, a graceful doe. Let her breasts fill you at all times with delight; be intoxicated always in her love. Why should you be intoxicated, my son, with a forbidden woman and embrace the bosom of an adulteress?" (Proverbs 5:18–20). I, as a husband, cannot take delight in anyone else's breasts. This means I can't look at porn or a lot of stuff on Instagram. I can't have an affair. I can't gawk on the beach or at the TV. I can't linger on social media. This is one way to look at those verses, and it is correct. However, this is a positive statement, not a negative one. Why try to act like this isn't a good thing? There is no shame in taking delight in your wife's breasts. Ladies, there is no shame in taking delight in your husband's . . . twinkle in his eyes. I am free to delight in my wife's breasts. It is not wrong or dirty. It is good. In fact, delighting in my wife's breasts is a special gift only for me. I am to be intoxicated always in her love.

My marriage is an amazing gift from God. It is a gift for both of us. I get all her love and affection, and she gets all of mine. I get her to believe in my dreams, and I get to believe in hers. I have someone who will stick with me through anything, and I will get to be the man who sticks with her no matter what. Marriage is given to us by God before the fall of man. Marriage is good. Success is to delight in your life with your spouse. This seems like an easier and more attainable goal than many of the things Solomon was chasing.

How do we live successfully on this earth? We obey God and enjoy the life he has given us. This is what Solomon teaches us. This makes sense when you look at the fruit of the Spirit. We all want peace and joy. The only way to get lasting peace or lasting joy is through the Spirit working in us and producing fruit. We can't force peace or joy in our lives. We can't find peace or joy anywhere else. We can't get peace or joy from money, a career, social media, or anything else. Therefore, without obeying God those items are impossible to attain. The world can't get those. You and I can't get those following any path in this world. Solomon proves this. We only get them with obedience to God. We obey God in all ways and at all times, and then we are free to enjoy what comes from faithful obedience.

Lastly, we are told, "whatever your hand finds to do, do it with all your might." This also seems to apply to the parable of the talents. Two of the servants do their work well and are rewarded. The last servant doesn't and is called lazy and wicked. Whenever I think of the joy of hard work, I think of the first funeral I ever performed.

This funeral was at the little church in the little town. The man who had died was well respected by everyone in the community. He was a lifelong farmer and by all accounts a tremendous man guided by his strong faith in God. He ate and drank with a thankful heart. He celebrated things that were truly worthy of being celebrated. He enjoyed life with his spouse as she enjoyed life with him. Here is how I opened his funeral service:

In Genesis 2:15, we see that the Lord God took the man and put him in the garden of Eden to work it and take care of it. Has ever a Bible verse fit a man better than this one? In the beginning God created the earth and he created man to tend his garden. God created this world to reflect his creativity and beauty and to provide for us. Much of Maurice's life involved tending God's earth. There is a special relationship between God and a farmer. Farming is about faith the crops will come, patience the rain will come, and persistence in bringing in the harvest. Just last fall Maurice was out driving his combine. I don't know if there is a harvest in heaven. I believe there is because I know we have work to do there. In the garden of Eden man was made to take care of the crops and the animals. Then there is the fall of man as we rebel against God. The rest of the Bible is then all about God's redemption of his people. The capstone is the arrival of God on earth in Jesus. Jesus takes our sin, shame, and blame upon himself and forgives us through his death. He redeems us through his resurrection when he came back from death. Then in the last few chapters of the Bible Jesus makes all things new and God returns to his people. "Then the angel showed me the river of the water of life, as clear as crystal, flowing from the throne of God and of the Lamb down the middle of the great street of the city. On each side of the river stood the tree of life, bearing twelve crops of fruit, yielding its fruit every month. And the leaves of the tree are for the healing of the nations. The river waters and the tree produces fruit each month" (Revelation 22:1–). This sounds and awful like farming to me. The love of the land and the skills developed throughout his life are serving Maurice well in heaven. This simple man knew how to live a successful life.

God graciously gives a work to do, and we find life as we do the work with all our hearts. This is exactly where the one-talent servant fails and finds himself thrown into hell. He doesn't do the work. The stark contrast of the master's reaction to his servants is highlighted here. It wasn't just that the one-talent servant was afraid of the master. It's that the one-talent servant didn't do what the master had told him to do. The master entrusted him with that gift, and it was never used. There was nothing to show for it. He truly wasted his life and was punished for it. There is no middle ground with the master's response. He either invites the servant in to share in his happiness, or he casts him out into a place of utter despair.

God has given something to all of us. He will come back to take account of what we have done with what he has given us. We will either be rewarded in the best way possible or punished in the worst way possible. Can I miss out on heaven because I am too selfish on earth? Does Jesus reinforce this idea in Matthew 7:21 when he says, "Not everyone who says to me, 'Lord, Lord,' will enter the kingdom of heaven, but only the one who does the will of my Father who is in heaven"? I don't think so. I am saved by Jesus. I repented of my sins and was baptized to signify that I have died to myself to live for Jesus. Jesus is the one who saves. In the parable, I think Jesus brought us to the master, the master gave the talents, and the Holy Spirit guides us to use the talent for the glory of the master. But what do I know?

To get back to the servants being successful, a verse Psalm 37:4 perfectly encapsulates this: "Take delight in the Lord, and he will give you the desires of your heart." First you delight in the Lord.

You don't try and delight anywhere else. Delight in anything else will prove to be a dead end because anything else is not God. Only God is perfectly delightful. We look to him for what we need, and he will give it. That is what Solomon describes in Ecclesiastes 9. He states that your food, drink, spouse, and work are all great gifts from God. So go out there and enjoy them. However, don't try to find your delight in any of those. First, delight in God, and then you will find your peace, joy, and contentment. Those other places (food, drink, spouse, work) are not designed to give you peace, joy, contentment, or success. Your success is this—God is delightful, and he called to you.

CHAPTER 10

This Still Doesn't Seem Fair

D id you skip to this chapter? Be honest. At some point in this book, you couldn't shake the feeling this whole thing just isn't fair. How did God choose who to give more and who to give less? Why didn't I get a rocket arm so I could play professional sports? Why has God chosen me to bless with so . . . little? Well, let's make it worse before we get to the answer.

Jesus talks about three servants in the parable of the talents. One of them receives something like $42 million in today's numbers. He goes out and uses $42 million to gain another $42, million. So, when the master comes back, this man can report back to him, "Hey, I doubled your money. It is now $84 million." To which his master replied, "Well done, good and faithful servant. You have been faithful over a little; I will set you over much. Enter into the joy of your master." So what's wrong with this? Well, there is another servant who got $108 million. And he was able to go out and double his too. He started with more and was able to bring even more in.

Say it with me, "that's not fair!" It gets worse—he gave them these amounts based on their ability! It was not even random. He knew these two servants and knew one could handle more than the other. Now, if you and I put ourselves in the place of the servants and say the master is God, I think it gets almost too hard to swallow. I believe God made us. So, did he make me with less ability than someone else? Why would God make people with varying abilities? Why aren't we all created equal? Why am I a loser working at a small church and that other person is a winner working at a huge church that he or she started?

Why is this a wrong way to look at it? Well, because, once again, I am looking at myself as the hero in the parable. Remember what Rick Warren wrote? It's not about you. I think I'm the hero in this story. I'm not. The parable is used to teach me about God and his kingdom. To get a grasp on this question, I think we need to examine the parable of the laborers in the vineyard found in Matthew 20:1–16:

> For the kingdom of heaven is like a master of a house who went out early in the morning to hire laborers for his vineyard. After agreeing with the laborers for a denarius a day, he sent them into his vineyard. And going out about the third hour he saw others standing idle in the marketplace, and to them he said, "You go into the vineyard too, and whatever is right I will give you." So, they went. Going out again about the sixth hour and the ninth hour, he did the same. And about the eleventh hour he went out and found others standing. And he said to them, "Why do you stand here idle all day?" They said to him, "Because no one has hired us." He said to them, "'You go into the vineyard too." And when evening came, the owner of the vineyard said to his foreman, "Call the laborers and pay them their wages, beginning with the last, up to the first." And when those hired about the eleventh hour came, each of them received a denarius. Now when those hired first came, they thought they would receive more, but each of them also received a denarius. And on receiving it they grumbled at the master of the house, saying, "These last worked only one hour, and you have made them equal to us who have borne the burden of the day and the scorching heat." But he replied to one of them, "Friend, I am doing you no wrong. Did you not agree with me for a denarius? Take what belongs to you and go. I choose to give to this last worker as I give to you. Am I not allowed to do what I choose with what belongs to me? Or do you begrudge my generosity?" So the last will be first, and the first last.

How much more unfair can this be?

We can focus on the vineyard owner saying "What business is it of yours what I pay people? You needed work and I gave you work. I was generous with you. You were happy to find work and get paid this amount until others worked less hours than you. Don't like what I did there? Go and build your own vineyard if you care about this so much. Oh wait, you can't build your own vineyard. That's what I thought. You're welcome." This is my interpretation. It's the wrong one. Well, it isn't completely wrong. However, the vineyard owner isn't sarcastic in the original text. The gist is the same. It is his vineyard, not theirs. He graciously went out to hire people who needed work. He graciously kept going out all day to find more workers. He made sure they knew what they were going to be paid, so he was not trying to take advantage of them. He was honest.

Where did the problem come? It came from the workers thinking things aren't fair. If we continue the human line of thought, then we could start to build a case they should be paid differently based on how much they worked. Maybe instead of paying a salary, the owner should have paid hourly or by amount of work done. The owner doesn't do it this way. This bothers us. It shouldn't though. It's none of our business. You and I can't help ourselves from sticking our noses where they don't belong. This isn't our vineyard. The owner of the vineyard pays a very fair wage. He isn't taking advantage of anyone. We just get frustrated because it doesn't seem fair. However, this is a parable. The owner is God. There is the rub. God is perfect, and we all deserve death. The idea he would even come down to us and invite us to be a part of his kingdom is unfathomable. The idea we would then be ungrateful should be laughable.

In these two parables of Jesus, we learn that what we think is fair or unfair pales in comparison to the amazing grace of God. Let's not pretend that we are good workers. We lie, cheat, steal, and shop on Amazon during our shift. We are guilty. We cannot stand up to judgment. We deserve nothing from God. What he has given to us is all because of his grace. We should be gushing with thankfulness that he came into the marketplace to give us work and a paycheck. We had no hope, and he came to us. You and I are nothing without God. There is nothing without God. How can I be so brazen or unaware that I would be upset with anything in my life when everything is God's gift? This would be like me buying my child a car and him or her complaining that their friend's car is better. I wouldn't only be sad that I am unable to purchase a better car, but I would be broken that my child is so ungrateful.

I can still remember when my dad surprised me with a car. It was ugly, rusty, slow, and I was in love.[41] I didn't have to save up to buy a car. My dad bought me a car. Wow! Gratefulness is the only acceptable reaction to a gift given from the heart. With God we see a perfect master in perfect love giving gifts to ungrateful, sinful, undeserving people. Those three servants from the parable of the talents didn't deserve the talents. They didn't earn them. They simply received them from a great master.

But really, whose talents were they? Did the money given to the servants become theirs, or did it remain the master's money? The master decided to give obscene amounts of money to three different servants according to their abilities. This isn't a silent benefactor just giving stuff away. The master sounds more like a great coach. What makes a great coach? Getting the best out of their players for the benefit of the players and ultimately the team. The coach gets to know what their players can and cannot do. She sees the players' strengths and weaknesses and helps to get them in position to do the best they can. The master gave the talents to the servants based on their abilities. That is another incredible example of God's grace with us.

At the turn of the century[42] the Los Angeles Lakers had two of the all-time greatest basketball players—Shaquille O'Neal and Kobe Bryant. They might be among the ten greatest to ever play the game. If we were looking at talents, they would both be five-talent servants. However, they were very different players. Shaq was huge and stronger than everyone else. He wasn't just sort of stronger, he was significantly stronger. He was also incredibly athletic. Kobe was confidence wearing a jersey. He wasn't just a skilled shooter. Kobe is widely considered as the greatest closer in the history of basketball. If you had one person to take a shot to win the game, most of us would pick Kobe over the likes of even Michael Jordan or Steph Curry. Why? It's just who he was. You knew he was going to rise to the occasion and make the game winner. At the end of the game, would their coach Phil Jackson set up a play for Shaq to hit a three pointer? No. This would be an unbelievably terrible move.[43] Shaq is in the discussion as one of the most game-changing players of all time, yet he was not a three-point shooter. If his coaches told him to not go to the basket but to stay out and shoot three-point shots, you and I wouldn't even know his name. A good coach knows his or her players' abilities. The coach sets up their players for success, creating the best opportunities for them to succeed.

Again, the master gave the servants talents based on their abilities. God knows us perfectly and knows exactly how we can be best used in his kingdom. I can assume the master gave the two-talent servant the two talents because three, four, or five talents would have been outside of his expertise. Maybe giving this servant three or four or even the coveted five talents would have broken him. Ephesians 2:10 states, "For we are God's handiwork, created in Christ Jesus to do good works, which God prepared in advance for us to do." There is a work God has created me to do. Why would I assume he won't help me with it? Why would I think he wouldn't equip me for it? Conversely, why would I assume it is not good enough? Why would I think I need to do something more important than the work he has created me to do? But I do think that.

I've heard it said "God gives everyone one hundred. We all just get it in different proportions." At one point I had adopted that saying as a philosophy in my life. It means I look at someone who seems to be doing better in an area of life and assume I must be doing better in a different area. The best illustration I can think of is driving past mansions and telling your kids, "Well we don't live in a mansion, but I'm a better father than all those guys." The assumption is they are only good at making money. Since I don't have as much money, I must be a better father. It is faulty and dangerous thinking. In fact, the idea we all get one hundred but in different proportions for different people is dangerous. First, it's not true. Truth is pretty important. Second, this thinking tempts me to judge other people and compare myself to them. That helps no one. Ephesians 2:10 gives me a much clearer understanding of God's truth. I am a creation of God. He created me to do good works. He prepared those in advance for me to do. There is no comparison in his philosophy. Once again, God's truth is life-giving, not life-stealing.

Paul writes about this in 1 Corinthians 12:21–27.

> The eye cannot say to the hand, "I don't need you!" And the head cannot say to the feet, "I don't need you!" On the contrary, those parts of the body seem to be weaker are indispensable, and the parts we think are less honorable we treat with special honor. And the parts that are unpresentable are treated with special modesty, while our presentable parts need no special treatment. But God has put the body together, giving greater honor to the parts that lacked it, so that there should be no division in the body, but that its parts should have equal concern for each other. If one part suffers, every part suffers with it; if one part is honored, every part rejoices with it. Now you are the body of Christ, and each one of you is a part of it.

I guess instead of writing this entire book I could have just written 1 Corinthians 12:27 on a piece of paper and given it to you for free. Perhaps it would be much healthier for you and me to realize we are included in the body of Christ than to wonder why we aren't a different part of body.

Why the book, then? Well, I had read this verse several times during my years of pride, jealousy, and burying my talent in the ground. Every time I read this verse, I wondered what it would feel like to be something unimportant, because I was felt that I was obviously something important. I'm correct, but not in the way I wanted to be. I am important because God gave me a work to do. I am not important if I'm comparing myself to others. Someone said, "comparison is the thief of joy." I'd add that comparison has no upside. There is no value in comparing myself to others. There is a work for me to do and it is a part of the larger body of Christ. It is far more fruitful for me to focus my attention on doing work than to wonder if I'm a success or a failure.

CHAPTER 11

Success or Failure?

A m I success or a failure? It is the tough question I ask myself. You probably ask yourself this as well. It's probably why you bought this book. It is natural. This is the question that many of struggle with most. I feel like I spend way too much time thinking about this. It has gotten better over time, but it still lingers in my thoughts. I don't think it has to do with how long the time is though. I think it gets better as I continue to walk in obedience to God. Success and failure seem to be less important in the light of God's love and will. I used to think about it nonstop. I would wake up and go to sleep wondering if I was more successful than others at my age or why I was less successful than the guy down the street. Now I see I was really worshiping myself and not worshiping God. I was interested in leaving my mark on the world and not the master's. I was interested in what others thought of me. I wanted everyone to see me as successful. To reach back into the Old Testament, I was far more like King Saul than King David. In chapter 9 we looked at King Saul and how he was the epitome of looking successful. He was tall and handsome. He looked the part. He probably even sounded the part. But he ended up losing everything in disgrace. The entire kingdom was handed over, by God, to David. The two of them couldn't have been more different.

All we need to do is look at how each of them is introduced to us in the Bible. Dare I call it their origin story?[44] Here is the biblical record of our introductions to these two men.

Saul: "There was a Benjamite, a man of standing, whose name was Kish son of Abiel, the son of Zeror, the son of Bekorath, the son of Aphiah of Benjamin. Kish had a son named Saul, as handsome a young man as could be found anywhere in Israel, and he was a head taller than anyone else" (1 Samuel 9:1–2). Saul is the handsome and tall son of a man of standing. There is little else needed to picture this man in my mind. From a worldly standpoint, he has it all.

David: His story is the polar opposite. It starts with the Lord telling the prophet Samuel to go to Jesse's house. The whole town was afraid when he showed up. The story picks up here in 1 Samuel 16:4–12

> Samuel did what the Lord said. When he arrived at Bethlehem, the elders of the town trembled when they met him. They asked, "Do you come in peace?" Samuel replied, "Yes, in peace; I have come to sacrifice to the Lord. Consecrate yourselves and come to the sacrifice with me." Then he consecrated Jesse and his sons and invited them to the sacrifice.
>
> When they arrived, Samuel saw Eliab and thought, "Surely the Lord's anointed stands here before the Lord." But the Lord said to Samuel, "Do not consider his appearance or his height, for I have rejected him. The Lord does not look at the things people look at. People look at the outward appearance, but the Lord looks at the heart." Then Jesse called Abinadab and had him pass in front of Samuel. But Samuel said, "The Lord has not chosen this one either." Jesse then had Shammah pass by, but Samuel said, "Nor has the Lord chosen this one." Jesse had seven of his sons pass before Samuel, but Samuel said to him, "The Lord has not chosen these." So he asked Jesse, "Are these all the sons you have?" "There is still the youngest," Jesse answered. "He is tending the sheep." Samuel said, "Send for him; we will not sit down until he arrives." So he sent for him and had him brought in. He was glowing with health and had a fine appearance and handsome features. Then the Lord said, "Rise and anoint him; this is the one."

Let's get this straight. David's dad doesn't even think he is good enough to be listed with his brothers to be considered as king. That may be the only thing we need to know about David to understand how much different he is than Saul. David is tending the sheep. Shepherding in that day was done by the most "loserly" person around or in the family. This was obviously young David.

Saul is tall and handsome, and his father is of good standing. David is short, still handsome, and his father is a joke. Seriously, King Saul called him the son of Jesse as an insult. Their introductions as king couldn't have been more different if this was fiction. They are perfectly at odds with each other. Saul is successful looking. Saul is Leo in the *Wolf of Wall Street*. Saul comes from success. It makes sense this would happen for Saul. His granite jaw will look wonderful on our coins. He looks like a king we can be proud of. David is the polar opposite. David doesn't look like a king. In fact, at one point David marries Saul's daughter,[45] and she says he doesn't even act like a king.[46] The differences don't stop there. They run much deeper.

David doesn't seem to worry about his legacy or perceived success. One such example of this is when he builds a great house for himself and then feels terrible that he didn't build one for God. God makes it clear he doesn't want David to build his house. So what does David do? He spends the rest of his life collecting all the items needed to build a great palace for God. He has joy serving God, knowing that he won't even get to see the completion of his work. In this way his son can have everything ready for it. Even when David is anointed king, he continues to serve Saul. Saul tries to kill him repeatedly, and he still serves Saul as king and makes sure his own men don't hurt Saul. David honors God by honoring Saul. Then of course we see David's heart in full display in the Psalms. The following list was compiled by Ron Edmonson in an article entitled "10 Reasons David is called a Man after God's own Heart."[47]

David is humble: "Lowborn men are but a breath, the highborn are but a lie; if weighed on a balance, they are nothing; together they are only a breath" (Psalm 62:9). Saul was not humble. He started off scared and full of anxiety. Then he became important and scared and full of anxiety. He made decisions because he was afraid of the people

David is reverent: "I call to the Lord, who is worthy of praise, and I am saved from my enemies" (Psalm 18:3). Saul literally builds a monument to himself.

David is respectful: "Be merciful to me, O Lord, for I am in distress; my eyes grow weak with sorrow, my soul and my body with grief" (Psalm 31:9). Saul lies to the prophet when confronted.

David is trusting: "The Lord is my light and my salvation—whom shall I fear? The Lord is the stronghold of my life—of whom shall I be afraid?" (Psalm 27:1). Again, Saul was afraid. He feared people far more than he feared God.

David is loving: "I love you, O Lord, my strength" (Psalm 18:1). There is no evidence in the Bible Saul loved God. None.

David is devoted: "You have filled my heart with greater joy than when their grain and new wine abound" (Psalm 4:7). God was not enough for Saul.

David recognizes God's work: "I will praise you, O Lord, with all my heart; I will tell of all your wonders" (Psalm 9:1). Saul looked for people to praise him. He wanted to do wonderful things.

David is faithful: "Surely goodness and love will follow me all the days of my life, and I will dwell in the house of the Lord forever" (Psalm 23:6). Saul was worried about his kingdom. He didn't want to be king, not originally. He was afraid and hid. Then he immediately started building up his kingdom using his own power.

David is obedient: "Give me understanding, and I will keep your law and obey it with all my heart" (Psalm 119:34). Saul is completely disobedient, and that's why he loses the kingdom.

David is repentant: For the sake of your name, O Lord, forgive my iniquity, though it is great" (Psalm 25:11). Saul never admitted wrong. He was a liar and a blamer.

Well, where do you fall? I sure feel like Saul. David and Saul are perfect examples of the battle of the flesh and the Spirit. I think this list is a wonderful explanation of what our flesh wants versus what the Spirit can give us. The difference between the two lists? It can be summed up in two words: faithful obedience. Saul continues to dig his own grave through fear, self-reliance, and lies. These are the things I do when I feel as though I'm not living up to the success I think I should have. I rationalize everything. I lie to myself. It is just a silly as saying my clothes are shrinking in the wash. No, Tim, your clothes are not shrinking. You are gaining weight, and it is completely because of what you are doing and not doing. David admits his problems and failures, and then he is open to the work of God in his life. Saul doesn't have the courage to see who he really is, and with that he cuts the work of God out of his life. David sees who he really is. Do I see who I really am? Do you see who you really are? How do we know who we really are? David writes about this in Psalm 139.

> O Lord, you have searched me and known me!
> You know when I sit down and when I rise up;
> you discern my thoughts from afar.
> You search out my path and my lying down
> and are acquainted with all my ways.
> Even before a word is on my tongue,
> behold, O Lord, you know it altogether.
> You hem me in, behind and before,
> and lay your hand upon me.
> Such knowledge is too wonderful for me;
> it is high; I cannot attain it. (Psalm 139:1–6)

We know who we really are when open ourselves up to God. We delight in him. We confess to him. We speak with him. We play with him. We have a relationship with him as a child to a parent. Why? Because he knows us. He teaches us. God is our Father. Like in Psalm 23:3, he guides us along right paths. Like in John 10:10, he gives us life and life to the fullest. It's when we are in an honest relationship with God that can we see who we really are.

If I'm a two-talent servant, it's best for me to come to that real-ization and not try to be a five-talent servant. If Shaq tried to be Kobe, he would never have been Shaq and revolutionized basket-ball. He wouldn't have even made the NBA. If Kobe had tried to play Shaq's game, he would have just been pushed around by much big-ger guys. Kobe sliced and diced with the skill of a surgeon because he knew what he was good at. Saul was trying to be a five-talent servant. He looked the part and tried to act the part. Could he have been a great king? Certainly! It's there in the Bible. It's all over the Bible, especially in the Old Testament. There are multiple places where the simple axiom is laid out: "Do what I say, and you will be blessed. Don't do it and you will be cursed." That never disap-peared in the New Testament either. It's still a solid way to live. Saul wouldn't listen to the coach. Saul did not listen to the master. He buried his opportunity in the ground. Just like the one-talent servant, he was afraid. To ask how many talents were given to Saul or to David is a faulty question that doesn't keep in line with the intent of the parable. The five-talent and two-talent servants don't question what they have. They go out and use it for the master's glory. The big difference between the two seems to be their rela-tionship with God.

David writes this in Psalm 139:23–24: "Search me, O God, and know my heart! Try me and know my thoughts! And see if there be any grievous way in me and lead me in the way everlasting!" David was very coachable. David believed that the master gave him talents based on his abilities. This picture is painted masterfully when we read the account of his battle with Goliath in 1 Samuel 17.

The Israelites and the Philistines are in a war. At that time, a common way to battle was for each side to send out one fighter to represent the entire army. Both sides would agree that they would honor the rules and walk away if their warrior lost the one-on-one battle. This cut down on a significant loss of life for both sides. The Philistines sent out Goliath. He was so large that he intimated the entire Israelite army. For forty days they sat there as he came out to challenge and mock them. He was a worldly five-talent guy, and the Israelites did not believe they had someone with the ability to fight him and win. David came out to bring food to his brothers and was shocked at what Goliath was yelling. He couldn't believe what was going on. He went out to fight Goliath. He knew he would win the fight because he knew God would judge Goliath and give victory to the Israelites.

I don't believe that David placed his faith in himself or his own abilities. I think he just knew that God wasn't looking for a winner; he was looking for someone willing to be his vessel. David's success came because of his faithful obedience to God. How was David so confident? He knew that God would give him what he needed according to his abilities. In this case, the ability was to sling a stone like he had done multiple times while tending sheep. I'm certain that there were many men there who could have done the same thing but lacked the faith in God to do it. I would guess that David wasn't even the best at it. Slinging a stone would have been an incredibly common skill at that time, and I'm sure that most of those warriors could have done the same thing David did. But they didn't. David did. David knew God and asked God to help him know himself. When David prayed for success, he did it for God's glory and not his own. I, on the other hand, like Saul, crave success for myself, my own glory, and my own ego.

Instead of seeing David as a giant killer, what if we saw him the same as the young boy who offered his lunch to Jesus to feed thousands of people in John 6? In that story Jesus wants to feed thousands of people and tells his disciples to do it. They can't figure out how, so one of them speaks up in verses 8–9: "Another of his disciples, Andrew, Simon Peter's brother, spoke up, 'Here is a boy with five small barley loaves and two small fish, but how far will they go among so many?'" You've probably never read that story and thought, "Wow that kid is amazing! He performed a miracle and was able to feed all those people with just his lunch!" We never do that because it's obvious in this story that Jesus did it. The kid just happens to be there with a lunch that his mom packed. He probably has a sweater too just in case it gets chilly.

Yet we read about David and Goliath and give David a bunch of credit. David is explicit when in 1 Samuel 17:37: "The Lord who rescued me from the paw of the lion and the paw of the bear will rescue me from the hand of this Philistine." Then in verses 45–47 he shouts this to Goliath in the hearing of all those gathered there, "

> You come against me with sword and spear and javelin, but I come against you in the name of the Lord Almighty, the God of the armies of Israel, whom you have defied. This day the Lord will deliver you into my hands, and I'll strike you down and cut off your head. This very day I will give the carcasses of the Philistine army to the birds and the wild animals, and the whole world will know that there is a God in Israel. All those gathered here will know that it is not by sword or spear that the Lord saves; for the battle is the Lord's, and he will give all of you into our hands.

David gives all the credit to God working through him. Yet, we see David as the one responsible for Goliath's death. Why don't we just see David as the servant whom God gave the talent based on his ability? That is how David saw himself, and that's why he puts his talents to use, as opposed to another man who was sitting there that day—Saul.

Of course, all this makes sense because we started right here in the first place. Right? The master gave each servant talents according to their ability. The master knew their ability. God knows your ability. God knows you. God knows me. I can doubt myself, constantly wondering if I'm a success or failure. It seems the master is not at all concerned about this. He tells both the five-talent and two-talent servant he is pleased with them. They both used what the master had given them to the best of their different abilities. They didn't get different rewards. They aren't labeled as mildly successful and super successful. The master wanted to know what they did with what they were given. This lends itself to two very important questions for all of us, whether we are five-talent, two-talent, or one-talent servants. What were you given? What are you doing with it?

CHAPTER 12

What Have You Done with What You Were Given?

What were you given? What are you doing with it?

In the parable all three servants were given something. It was not the same thing, and it didn't seem to bother any of them. It was not an important part of the teaching. The master simply gives them each an amount, and the only explanation for it was that it was based on their ability. He didn't speak of what they thought of what they were entrusted with. Jesus simply tells us what they produced. The important part of the story is they were entrusted with something and there was an expectation they would do something with it.

We must have a better understanding of what we have been given. I mean this in a very general sense. Jesus didn't go into specifics in the parable of the talents. He just has the number each servant received, and we've already established that the number was given based on the servant's ability. Occam's Razor[48] rings true here, as we can say that the simplest answer is probably the best. The servants were given something based on their abilities. Two of them doubled the something and one of them buried it and gave it back. In a general sense, we must know what we were given. I think we can also add that we should examine our ability as well.

I had a terrible understanding of what I was given. I thought I was given ten talents. Perhaps I thought I had the ability to have been given ten talents. I saw the people I would say were successful, and I knew I was one of them. I also assumed that the people I thought were successful were the people that God would say are successful. After all, some guy told me this at a camp when I was a little kid. It was reinforced to me throughout my years growing up. I had this illusion I was different and better than most others. What did this do for me? It ruined me. Absolutely nothing in the Bible agreed with my delusions of grandeur. But that didn't matter because I would read it into the story anyway. I was David in David and Goliath. Of course, the hero of the story is God. But to me, and many others, the hero was David. I was interested in doing great things for God. David didn't kill Goliath to do great things for God. He killed Goliath because he was found faithful and obedient so that God could do a great thing through him. I always had the emphasis on me doing the things, not God. This thinking led to problems.

I thought nothing was ever good enough for me. I looked at all the other pastors in my life and thought I was better than each one of them. Maybe I didn't think this completely, but I assumed with time I would get to be better than each one of them. Then over time my thinking started to sway the other way and I wondered if I simply was not as good as those other servants. I thought it's why I was at small churches. These extreme swings weren't God's fault. These extreme swings are the natural ends of this type of limited thinking. From what I know of Saul and David, I would have to guess that Saul felt the extremes of thinking he's awesome and thinking he's nothing while David would have been much more emotionally level as he saw God's will at work and not his own.

What was I given?

I was given the gift of life. This is where we all have to start, and it's possibly the place where we should spend the most time. I must be grateful for my life. God didn't have to do this. He didn't have to create me. He chose to. He also chose to give me the gift of grace. These two realizations are the foundations of reality. You are not an accident, because God created you. God loves you, and the evidence for that is his grace. The evidence of his grace is Jesus. Perhaps the two servants who did well were more interested in the love of and for the master than they were themselves. This is not a self-help book. We can't help ourselves. Only God can help us.

WHAT HAVE YOU DONE WITH WHAT YOU WERE GIVEN?

I was also given the Bible and numerous Bible teachers (from professors to neighbors) to help me see reality. It is too hard to list all I was given. Where do I start and when would I end this list? Health, family, gifts, experiences, culture, etc. This parable shows us we are given something. I was given my life in all it is beautiful messiness. Specifically, like the parable teaches, I was a servant of the master, and I was entrusted with something. I was to be faithful with it. There was a work for me to do. I was a part of the body of Christ. I had a role to play in his church. I had a role to play in his kingdom. I am invited into the master's story.

I don't live a life with personal shoppers and drivers. In fact, there are days if I showed up to the office and did absolutely nothing, no one would know.[49] I don't need to maximize my time or keep my eye out for decision fatigue. These realties don't make me any less of a servant than a servant who has to do those things. Humbly, I need to remember it also doesn't make me any better. The servants who did something with what the master gave them were both rewarded the same. The guy with a personal chef is a part of the same team as I, the guy who goes home for lunch most days, am.

What am I doing with it?

How do I begin to answer this question? Do I answer like Saul and try to list my accomplishments? Do I answer like David and say I'm doing what God wants . . . most of the time? These don't seem to fit well enough. I like what God says to Joshua after the death of Moses. Moses was a huge figure for the people. Joshua was a big deal, but not as big of a deal as Moses. If Joshua was a five-talent servant, Moses was a fifty-talent servant. However, Moses started off fearful. He definitely wanted to bury his talent in the ground.[50] He ran away. God dragged him back. Well, it's not entirely true. God called to him, and to his credit Moses did answer. It took work and the help of his brother, but he did decide to follow. Moses led well. Now it was Joshua's time to lead. At the beginning of the aptly named book of Joshua, God commissions Joshua. Here is part of what he says:

Only be strong and very courageous, being careful to do according to all the law Moses my servant commanded you. Do not turn from it to the right hand or to the left, you may have good success wherever you go. This Book of the Law shall not depart from your mouth, but you shall meditate on it day and night, so you may be careful to do according to all is written in it. For then you will make your way prosperous, and then you will have good success. (Joshua 1:7–8)

What am I supposed to be doing with God has given me? It's answered in this commission. I am supposed to succeed. Here's the catch. I don't succeed because of my greatness. I can only succeed when I follow the rest of this commission. I am supposed to be obedient to him. I am supposed to know his Word. I am supposed to follow his Word. I am supposed to carefully follow his Word. I am supposed to not turn from it to the right hand or to the left. If I do, then I will have good success wherever I go, and he will make my way prosperous. God's commission to Joshua is also his promise to Joshua.

Did I go too far? Does this really pertain to you and me? After all, this is God speaking to Joshua. It is God speaking to Joshua in the book of Joshua. Does this apply to us? I'll say yes and no. Does this specific case apply to you and me? No, neither of us are leading the people of Israel after the death of Moses. In that way this is specific to Joshua. In another way it can certainly apply to all of us called by God. This promise seems to be backed up in the New Testament and aimed at all Christians. In 2 Timothy 1:7 we read, "The Spirit God gave us does not make us timid, but gives us power, love and self-discipline." There are a few other verses (Acts 1:8, Matthew 10:28, Philippians 1:14, Matthew 28:20, and Hebrews 13:5) that reinforce this idea. However, I believe this one verse is enough to make the case. The last word is the telling one. The Spirit God gave us—gives us—self-discipline. It is what God is reinforcing to Joshua. Joshua needs to stay connected to the law and follow it.

This means that Joshua needs to know the law. He needs to set up his life to make sure he knows the law. That could be anything from writing on index cards and putting them on his bathroom mirror or hiring priests to sit in all of his meetings and strategy sessions to make sure he doesn't unknowingly break the law. Joshua must remain faithfully obedient to God and know the law. If he does, he will do well. For us, this promise may be truer. We aren't left with the just the law. We have many advantages over Joshua. We have the rest of the Bible. We have the example of Jesus. We are given the Spirit of God to help us follow him in faithful obedience.

What am I supposed to do with God has given me? Follow him in faithful obedience all the days of my life. It Paul's charge to Timothy. It is the words I will give you at the finish of this book. You have been given life. You have been given a chance to use it. You will be judged with what you have done with it. You will not be judged according to human definitions of success or failure. You will be judged according to the master's values. You cannot survive this judgment without Jesus Christ. His death and resurrection are paramount to your life and mine.

To really answer the question of what we're supposed to do with what God has given us, let's head to the verses preceding the parable of the vineyard owner we looked at in chapter 10. Jesus had mentioned twice previously that he would die, but this is the first time he gives details. Matthew 20:17–19 states, "as Jesus was going up to Jerusalem, he took the twelve disciples aside, and on the way he said to them, 'See, we are going up to Jerusalem. And the Son of Man will be delivered over to the chief priests and scribes, and they will condemn him to death and deliver him over to the Gentiles to be mocked and flogged and crucified, and he will be raised on the third day.'" This sets the scene for the huge twist as well as the answer to our questions in this final chapter of the book.

It happens with this lady. In Matthew 20:20–21 we read that "the mother of the sons of Zebedee came up to [Jesus] with her sons, and kneeling before him she asked him for something. And he said to her,

'What do you want?' She said to him, 'Say that these two sons of mine are to sit, one at your right hand and one at your left, in your kingdom.'" It's a sharp turn. Jesus speaks of the otherworldly grace and fairness of his Father. He then tells of the otherworldly love and sacrifice of his impending death. Then two disciples and their mommy come up and request positions of authority and prestige. Perhaps they weren't quite getting it. Warren Wiersbe sums it up wonderfully like this: "Jesus spoke about a cross, but they were interested in a crown."[51]

So am I. Well, I'm tempted to be interested in a crown instead of a cross. It is back when I thought it was okay to believe I was a ten-talent servant. I didn't quite grasp the definition of the word "servant." They didn't either. Wiersbe goes on to write, "The word *minister* in Matthew 20:26 means 'a servant.' Our English word 'deacon' comes from it. The word *servant* in Matthew 20:27 means 'a slave.' Not every servant was a slave, but every slave was a servant. It is sad to note in the church today that we have many celebrities, but very few servants. There are many who want to "exercise authority" (Matt. 20:25), but few who want to take the towel and basin and wash feet."[52] They wanted the glory of being in Jesus's posse. It tempts me too! I'm sure it tempts you as well. I want to be the famous pastor to Justin Bieber who has abs.[53] I want people to think I'm successful and great. Worse, I want to think I'm successful and great. I am tempted to care more about feeling successful than being successful in God's eyes. However, thinking like this is completely countercultural to the kingdom of heaven. I don't know how to say it stronger. It is completely the wrong attitude. Yet it is the attitude that is rewarded and reinforced. It is not okay to say it, but even Christians learn that they are supposed to try and gain the whole world.

Jesus answers the mother's request in Matthew 20:22–23, ""'You do not know what you are asking. Are you able to drink the cup I am to drink?' They said to him, 'We are able.' He said to them, 'You will drink my cup, but to sit at my right hand and at my left is not mine to grant, but it is for those for whom it has been prepared by my Father.'"

It is amazing to see Jesus answer them in such a loving way. There was a rebuke, but there was also grace. It is the same as my prayer into that stick twenty-five years ago. I was praying for my kingdom to fade and Jesus's kingdom to rise. It is as though Jesus was listening and thinking, "Oh, I will answer your prayer, Tim. I won't answer it how you think it should be answered. I will answer it in a way that will bring me glory and give you the honor of serving in my kingdom."

Then Jesus explains his answer further. This is how we can answer these questions: What was I given? What am I doing with it?

> But Jesus called them to him and said, "You know the rulers of the Gentiles lord it over them, and their great ones exercise authority over them. It shall not be so among you. But whoever would be great among you must be your servant, and whoever would be first among you must be your slave, even as the Son of Man came not to be served but to serve, and to give his life as a ransom for many. (Matthew 20:25–28)

Perhaps the servant who was given five talents was more humble, more broken, had a bigger heart, and was more interested in serving the master than the servant who was given two talents. Perhaps the servant's ability was his or her faithfulness and openness to the will of the master. What a twist that would be. Isn't that just the type of twist that would be in the kingdom of the King who stooped down to his subjects and became servant of them all? Wouldn't that be expected of the servant of the King who chose to live as a slave and die for his people? How dare we think that God would want us to be "awesome" in the world's standards? The greatest success a person can have is to be a faithful servant to the King of kings. That's it. That's not just it. That's incredible.

Remember how this book started off? "You don't get your lunch delivered to you so you can maximize your time?" We shared a good laugh about it. There is a well-known megachurch pastor who shares tips on how to use your time better, and this is one of them. He also suggests having someone pick out your clothes, so you don't get decision fatigue. I'm not making fun of this guy. Clearly, he has accomplished some wonderful things. It brings me back to one of the first "pastor" books I read where the guy said he got a limo and a driver so he could use his commuting time to the max.

However, now as a somewhat pudgy guy in his forties working at a small church, I don't wish for the life.

Why?

I'm a two-talent person.

I'm not a five-talent person.

I'm a two-talent person thanking God he only gave me what I had the ability to handle. Wow! He loves me and cares about me. He has set me up for success.

God has set you up for success too. It doesn't matter how many talents you were given. Use them.

Endnotes

1 James Swanson, *Dictionary of Biblical Languages with Semantic Domains: Greek (New Testament)* (Oak Harbor: Logos Research Systems, Inc., 1997).

2 Yes, I'm referring to Craig Groeschel. He is awesome. Calm down.

3 Robert Shuler. You know, the Crystal Cathedral guy. Well, they used to own it. Look it up.

4 I was not expecting that. It's like joking with the doctor that you're fat and she's like, "well the medical term is obese. And yes, you are obese."

5 On the Bible app given to me and you and everyone in the whole world for free from a church where the lead pastor doesn't pick out his clothes or food.

6 I made a website before most churches had a website or saw value in one. Ha.

7 South Beach wasn't asking at that point.

8 Most creative sentence in the book. You're welcome.

9 And if you're thinking this sounds like they were setting up those poor campers to a life of multilevel marketing, you're probably right. If that gets you upset, please grab your essential oils and get a good whiff of the lavender. It's scientifically proven to calm you.

10 Or first chair, or lead in the play, or soloist, or sitting at pole position . . .

11 . . . or the big kahuna, number-one ranked, top chef . . .

12 Still not sure why I thought that was something to brag about. It was a Dodge Caravan. That's not even a Grand Caravan. Now I have a Honda Odyssey. That's something to brag about! It's only ten years old too.

13 It was a thing. Google "shirts with snaps in the 90s."

[14] I believe the stick prayer is mentioned in 3 Timothy.

[15] The book was *If It's Going to Be, It's Up to Me.* May also be found in 3 Timothy.

[16] Yup.

[17] Yes, I'm forty-three. If you are younger, maybe you pick someone from your era.

[18] Sarcasm.

[19] Yes, I did cause the crimp when I was replacing the fuel filter. There, I feel better.

[20] It's impossible because there is always something new to conquer.

[21] Philippians chapter 2. Look – I used a footnote for the right reason!

[22] http://timboyd.blogspot.com/2016/10/discouragement.html

[23] https://www.e2elders.org/shop/p/understanding–elder–governance.

[24] https://www.e2elders.org.

[25] I bestowed the certification. I will print it out when I see him.

[26] Have I mentioned I'm also a comedian? I am. Seriously. Look me up.

[27] The author of this book. Me.

[28] Well, all except one!!! Hahaha. Sorry. That was terrible.

[29] Told you I'm a Comedian.

[30] https://www.instagram.com/preachersnsneakers.

[31] Seventeen. It is seventeen. That's not bad. Maybe I could get thirty-four and hire someone to fill them all. Then I can just live off my seventeen and not do anything. Here I come Shark Tank!

[32] Warren W. Wiersbe, *The Bible Exposition Commentary*, vol. 1 (Wheaton, IL: Victor Books, 1996), 92.

[33] https://www.instagram.com/p/CP0MSOqnYEo/?utm_medium=copy_link.

[34] Nicholas Schmidle, "Richard Branson's Plan to Beat Jeff Bezos into Outer Space," *Daily Comment, The New Yorker*, July 9, 2021, https://www.newyorker.com/news/daily-comment/richard-

bransons-plan-to-beat-jeff-bezos-to-outer-space.

35 Tim Herd with Colin Cowherd, "Why Beauty Matters at the Quarterback Position," *Fox Sports Radio*, November 1, 2019, https://foxsportsradio.iheart.com/content/2019-11-01-why-beauty-matters-at-the-quarterback-position/.

36 https://www.oxfordify.com/meaning/penitence

37 I could write much more about how delicious meat is. Vegan? Take a nap. I'm sure you're low on energy.

38 And it's our friend's boat. We don't have the money for a boat.

39 I know what you're thinking . . . there are more.

40 Can you imagine texting seven hundred people "Lunch was good? You?" every single day?

41 Chevy Citation—Why was it called a Citation? Because you should be cited for having such a cool car!!!!

42 Hard to believe it was the "turn of the century," huh? It was.

43 Almost as bad as throwing a pass when you could just hand the ball off to Marshawn Lynch for the touchdown.

44 I dare not.

45 Woah. Really? And you thought Thanksgiving was tough for you. Can you imagine that family dynamic?

46 2 Samuel 6:22. You know, the whole dancing in his underwear thing.

47 Ron Edmondson, "10 Reasons David Is Called 'A Man after God's Own Heart," *Bible Study Tools*, July 24, 2020, https://www.bible-studytools.com/bible-study/explore-the-bible/10-reasons-david-is-called-a-man-after-god-s-own-heart.html.

48 It's a thing.

49 Were you thinking you were the only one? Listen, I feel guilty about it too.

50 Like he buried that Egyptian! Zing!

51 Wiersbe, *The Bible Exposition Commentary*, 74.

52 Wiersbe, *The Bible Exposition Commentary*, 75.

53 Carl Lentz. Things aren't going very well for him anymore.

www.ingramcontent.com/pod-product-compliance
Lightning Source LLC
LaVergne TN
LVHW041200080426
835511LV00006B/679